*Mercier Press is the oldest independent Irish
publishing house and has published books in the
fields of history, literature, folklore, music, art,
humour, drama, politics, current affairs, law
and religion. It was founded in 1944 by John
and Mary Feehan.*

*In the building up of a country
few needs are as great as that of a publishing
house which would make the people proud of
their past, and proud of themselves as a people
capable of inspiring and supporting a world of
books which was their very own. Mercier Press
has tried to be that publishing house. On the
occasion of our fiftieth anniversary we thank
the many writers and readers who have
supported us and contributed to our success.*

*We face our second half-century
with confidence.*

# IRISH COUNTRY TOWNS

*Edited by*
**ANNGRET SIMMS**
*&*
**J. H. ANDREWS**

THE THOMAS DAVIS LECTURE SERIES
*General Editor: Michael Littleton*

*Published in association with*
RADIO TELEFÍS ÉIREANN

MERCIER PRESS

MERCIER PRESS
PO Box 5. 5 French Church Street, Cork
16 Hume Street, Dublin 2

© The Contributors, 1994

*A CIP is available for this book from the British Library*

ISBN 1 85635 088 6

10 9 8 7 6 5 4 3 2

## Acknowledgement

*The editor and publisher would like to thank the Ordnance Survey of Ireland for the maps based on the Ordnance Survey, by permission of the government [permit no. 5974] and the Ordnance Survey of Northern Ireland for the maps of Lurgan and Carrickfergus [permit no. 735], with the permission of the Controller of Her Majesty's Stationery Office.*

*Printed in Ireland by Colour Books Ltd.*

# CONTENTS

# LIST OF ILLUSTRATIONS

Kells from the south in 1820, by George Petrie (Thomas Cromwell, *Excursions through Ireland*)
Downpatrick, The Mall, 1863, by Thomas Semple, courtesy of Down County Museum
Carrickfergus, *c.* 1560 (British Library, Cotton Ms., Augustus I, ii, 42), courtesy of Royal Irish Academy
Maynooth, from the east-north-east in 1965 (J. K. St Joseph, Cambridge University Collection)
Enniscorthy in 1729 by William Munday (Hampshire County Record Office). Redrawn by Stephen Hannon
Bandon from the east in 1775 by Bernard Scalé (Devonshire estate papers. Chatsworth House, Derbyshire)
Lurgan, Main Street and Shankill parish church in 1905, courtesy of Ulster Museum, Belfast
Ennistymon and the River Cullenagh (Local Studies Centre)
Bray, Breslin's Marine Hotel, *c.* 1858 (National Library of Ireland)
Sligo in 1685 by Thomas Phillips (National Library of Ireland)
Athlone Castle in 1843 by F. W. Fairholt (Mr and Mrs S. C. Hall, *Ireland: its scenery, character, etc.*)
Shop-fronts in Dungarvan
Mullingar, market square in 1870, courtesy of Royal Irish Academy

# LIST OF MAPS

Kells, based on Ordnance Survey of Ireland, 1:2500, 1908-11, and *Irish Historic Towns Atlas,* courtesy of Royal Irish Academy, 1990
Downpatrick, based on Ordnance Survey of Northern Ireland, six inches to one mile, 1920
Carrickfergus *c.* 1840, *Irish Historic Towns Atlas,* 1986, courtesy of Royal Irish Academy
Maynooth 1838, Ordnance Survey of Ireland, six inches to one mile, railway added *c.* 1846
Enniscorthy 1939-40, Ordnance Survey of Ireland, six inches to one mile
Bandon 1938, Ordnance Survey of Ireland, 1:2500
Lurgan 1953-4, Ordnance Survey of Northern Ireland, six inches to one mile
Ennistimon 1916, Ordnance Survey of Ireland, six inches to one mile.
Castlecomer, based on Ordnance Survey of Ireland, six inches to one mile, 1902
Bray, based on Ordnance Survey of Ireland, six inches to one mile, 1937
Sligo, based on Ordnance Survey of Ireland, six inches to one mile, 1940, and Sligo City Development Plan 1992-1997
Athlone, based on Ordnance Survey of Ireland, six inches to one mile, 1952
Dungarvan, based on Ordnance Survey of Ireland, six inches to one mile, 1922-3
Mullingar 1953, Ordnance Survey of Ireland, 1:2500

# PREFACE

Ireland is a country of small towns. There are only six towns in the Republic with more that 25,000 inhabitants and most of the others have fewer than 5,000. Until fairly recently most of these small towns have had a bad press because prolonged economic depression dampened their spirits. But with the help of Bord Fáilte's scheme for Heritage Towns the mood has changed for the better.

Many of these small towns have long memories. Some, like Kells or Downpatrick, started when Gaelic-speaking monks built their monastery there in the early medieval period. Other places like Athlone and Carrickfergus began with Anglo-Norman lords who built powerful castles that still dominate the present towns. Sligo and Mullingar also belong to that medieval period. Then there are places like Enniscorthy or Lurgan, which were developed in the seventeenth century when planters from England and Scotland came to exploit Irish resources. Landed proprietors had a profound effect on places like Maynooth, Ennistymon and Castlecomer. Bray, as a seaside resort, represents the very small class of Irish towns that owe their urban status to the railway age. Each of these places tells the story of its townspeople through the layout of its streets and the choice of its street-names, its public buildings and the larger and smaller houses of merchants and artisans. The first chapter places the whole group in a more general historical context.

The Saw Doctors from Tuam are right when they stress the importance of our country towns. They are a signifcant aspect of our identity and a real force in shaping modern Irish men and women. They deserve to be better known. So next time, follow Professor Andrews's invitation at the beginning of his Mullingar narrative. His advice is not to speed through a town which you do not yet know. Park your car and start walking, not through the town but in the town. If you do so you will experience an intense appreciation of the passage of time and you will feel a bond with the past inhabitants of the town. You will begin to see behind the face of the present, because these towns blend space and time in a unique way. When you start asking yourself what is the oldest building in your town, then you have taken the first step towards appreciating how much previous generations have contributed towards shaping our present environment.

There is so much to discover about Irish towns that the Royal Irish Academy in Dublin decided to publish an *Irish Historic Towns Atlas*, in which the development of selected individual towns is traced in detail using both documentary materials and maps. Some of the country towns which we talk about here are already in print in the Academy series, namely Athlone, Bandon, Carrickfergus, Kells and Mullingar.

Following from the logic of the first chapter the sequence of the towns was chosen in chronological order by historical categories. It appeared important to include a town plan for every place and here I followed the principle of let a hundred flowers bloom. Where there were particularly attractive early maps, as for Carrickfergus and Enniscorthy, they were included; I am greatly indebted to Stephen Hannon from the Department of Geography in University College Dublin for drawing town plans which show the location of places mentioned in the text for those towns for which the ordnance survey maps appeared to be too cluttered.

This book is based on a Thomas Davis lecture series on Irish Country Towns which was broadcast by Radio Telefís Éireann between June and September 1991. I am very grateful to Michael Littleton, producer of the series, for his guidance to a succession of rather nervous university teachers, who are more accustomed to addressing a roomful of students than an invisible nation.

I would also like to thank Mercier Press in Cork for having adopted our town-series and in particular Maria O'Donovan, assistant editor, who was most encouraging and helpful right through the production stage. And most of all I am delighted and relieved that Professor J. H. Andrews, with whom as joint editor I began in 1985 the *Irish Historic Towns Atlas* series, offered his help with the texts. Anybody who knows his high editorial standards will realise how much the book benefited from his intervention.

*ANNGRET SIMMS*
*Department of Geography*
*University College Dublin.*

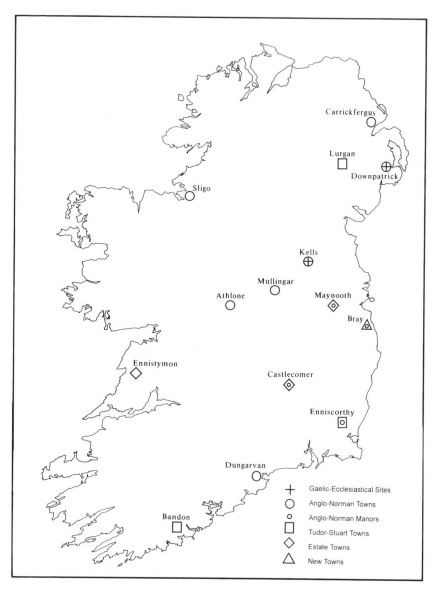

| | |
|---|---|
| + | Gaelic-Ecclesiastical Sites |
| ○ | Anglo-Norman Towns |
| ∘ | Anglo-Norman Manors |
| □ | Tudor-Stuart Towns |
| ◇ | Estate Towns |
| △ | New Towns |

*The location and origin of towns included in this book*

# THE ORIGIN OF IRISH TOWNS

## *Anngret Simms*

While the majority of townspeople in Ireland today live in urban agglomerations, by far the largest number of towns are those with a population of between 1,000 and 10,000 inhabitants. In the past our towns have contributed very little towards symbolising Irish identity. The political leaders of the first generation after the independence of the state evoked an image of Irish society which was almost exclusively rural. And indeed even today most postcards sent from Ireland show landscapes of wild cliffs along the coast, thatched cottages in green fields, empty roads with herds of cattle and sheep, Victorian pubs or perhaps an architectural landmark – seldom any urban landscape. It is hard to understand why this should be so, because towns are an important component in the history of a nation. They are important pointers in the search for historical identity. We can discover the story of our towns from the physical signs of their origin and development. The imprint of the past is particularly strongly expressed in the historic cores of our towns. The layout of the streets, the very street-names and public buildings, hold memories which are important for the inhabitants of that particular town, but they are also part of the story of the nation as a whole.

Think of each of these towns as a tangle of private and public passions, the desire of institutions, for example the churches, to assist people in their private lives but also to dominate them. Add to this the story of economic achievements and failures, as well as the spiritual paths of many individuals over the centuries, and you begin to realise the complexity of urban life. If we approach any of our towns with a questioning mind, then their fabric will turn into a living document in front of our eyes, recalling important chapters of defeat as well as occasional triumphs in the long history of the Irish people. Such stories are of great human interest, not only for those who live there but also for visitors.

Could it be that the past reluctance to accept towns as part of the Irish heritage that matters is related to the difficulty of defining our cultural identify? This is not a matter which we can brush aside as of no consequence because it affects our practical politics. It influences the answer to our question in whose image our towns were made and who ultimately contributed to the people who we are today.

Is it possible that the long neglect of Irish towns is related to the colonial history of our country? There is no doubt that, to a large extent, the formation of the urban network in Ireland was accelerated under the influence of repeated colonisation movements. In this, Ireland is not alone. There were other countries in Europe that were subject to colonisation during the middle ages, when a transition towards urbanisation was taking place. Medieval colonisation movements helped to spread cultural innovations and foremost among those was the idea of the chartered town, that is to say, the practice of granting settlements a specific town law. For a long time it was not appreciated in these countries that many of the present-day towns have roots that are firmly embedded in the pre-colonial past. This is true of Wales and Ireland where Anglo-Norman settlement was superimposed on the existing Celtic settlement. The same is true of the area east of the River Elbe in former East Germany and Poland, where medieval German settlements were superimposed on already existing West Slavic stronghold settlements. The reason why the formation of towns in countries which experienced colonisation movements was for so long solely associated with the newly planted colonial towns can partially be found in our understanding of the nature of towns. Almost until the middle of the twentieth century the study of urban origins was predominantly an aspect of legal and constitutional history. This approach produced a narrow definition of a town based on a specific town law and the formation of a municipal authority. The simple equation was that, without a charter, a settlement could not be considered a town. This very legalistic concept of a town hindered the assessment of the importance of earlier periods for the formation of towns.

This at last brings us to the important question: which were the formative periods of town formation in Ireland? As we have already hinted on the basis of archaeological and documentary evidence, we now know that there existed incipient towns or proto-towns in Ireland before the coming of the Anglo-Normans. The oldest towns in Ireland, dating to the later tenth and the eleventh centuries, are associated with either Gaelic monastic sites or Viking sea-ports, which date to the period between the ninth and the twelfth centuries; then follow the towns with a specific town law, which the Anglo-Normans introduced to Ireland. In fact, their colonisation, which began towards the end of the twelfth century, led directly to a century of new town building. The second important phase of new town building came after the reconquest of Ireland by the English with the plantations of the sixteenth and seventeenth centuries. These towns were primarily intended to be centres of anglicisation and to act as an insurance against future rebellions by the Irish. In the eighteenth century landlords initiated the building of estate towns; and during the nineteenth century we find a number of new towns as resorts or railway towns followed by a number of satellite towns which were established around the major urban centres of Dublin and Belfast in the twentieth century.

No doubt, towns were a tool in the hands of the colonisers with the intention to pacify and develop their newly conquered territories in military and economic as well as cultural terms. And in those circumstances it is not surprising that in the past the relationship between towns and their hinterlands was more often than not antagonistic. This would have been equally true for other parts of Europe where towns were developed by a colonising people, as for example medieval Danzig (present-day Gdansk in Poland), where the town was predominantly German in population while the hinterland was Polish.

One of the important features of Irish history is that the country was never part of the Roman Empire. Like Scandinavia, Scotland and the regions east of the River Elbe in Germany, Ireland was never directly influenced by Roman urban culture. The Celtic scholar D. A. Binchy described this situation very forcefully in a Thomas Davis lecture in 1953:

> *The example of Wales and Ireland shows that the urban civilisation which was transmitted to northern and western Europe through Graeco-Roman influence remained foreign to the Celtic-speaking peoples of these islands until it was more or less imposed on them by foreign conquerors.*

But in the light of more recent research it would appear that the early introduction of Christianity into Ireland transmitted many ideas from the Roman world, as the early-medieval Latin texts written in Ireland would suggest, and that the large Early Christian monasteries performed the functions of incipient towns. After all, the concept of a town as a cult site as well as a market place became one of the most powerful ideas which the medieval period inherited from the Roman world.

The Early Christian monasteries in Ireland played an important role as central places with far-reaching territorial connections. They fulfilled a variety of important functions. For example, the Columban monastery of Kells fulfilled educational functions. The religious houses taught the young in special schools. They were also patrons of the arts, as the beautiful high crosses at Kells show. They were keepers of treasures, for which they made good use of their round towers, and they granted sanctuary to those under persecution at a time when no government provided individuals with protection. They encouraged the development of a market place and they functioned as political centres. For example, Kildare was described by the seventh-century writer Cogitosus as the treasury of kings, while in the twelfth century Kells was the centre of the old Gaelic kingdom of Breifne.

Traces of these incipient towns are preserved in the

alignment of the modern street pattern, which as for example in Kells follows the curve of the outer and inner monastic enclosures containing the round tower, the stone crosses and the site of the medieval church and churchyard. The more secular part of the monastery was developed south-eastwards, where the market was held just outside the eastern gate. Kells is typical of other monastic sites like Armagh and Kildare which appear to have been designed in conformity with a planned arrangement. The round tower usually stands to the west of the church, where in moments of threat it could be reached quickly from the exit of the church. The entrance to the enclosure was generally located to the east and marked by a special cross, a boundary cross, around which market functions developed. It has been suggested that the concept of the market was brought into Ireland by the Vikings. But the historian Charles Doherty has emphasised that already before the Viking invasion an opportunity for the exchange of goods had developed in the form of the tribal *oenach*, or assembly, held on the borders of tribal territories. From the ninth century onwards, probably as the result of internal trade with the Vikings, some of the bigger monasteries took over the function of market places. The Irish word *margad* is a Scandinavian loan-word meaning market. By the eleventh century the major monasteries not only held markets but they also had paved streets, rows of houses and quarters for craftsmen.

The monastic towns constituted the cultural and economic power centres of early medieval Ireland when the Viking invasions began to haunt the country. From the ninth century onwards the Vikings began to establish coastal trading places and these developed very soon into important ports because of their long-distance trade, extending from Dublin in the west to Novgorod in the east. The Viking towns also greatly benefited from their rich Irish hinterland. They included Dublin, Waterford, Cork and Limerick with a few smaller ports like the walled Hiberno-Norse town of Wexford. It is astonishing how quickly these Viking settlements became so important that the economic life of the country was shifted permanently from the midlands to the coast and in particular to the east coast. No amount of regional planning in our time has so far been able to change this pattern.

Both the monastic towns and the Viking towns lacked a specific town law with an urban constitution. These attributes were to come with the institution of the town charter, which granted burgesses the privilege of self-government. The concept of a chartered town was borrowed from formerly Romanised Europe. The oldest known surviving town charter north of the Alps was issued in 1066, to Huy in present-day Belgium, interestingly enough near the present power-house of Europe. The constitutional ideas of the town charter establishing in part autonomous government for the burgesses were reflected in the town plan. The town walls expressed dramatically the need for communal protection. The town walls also symbolised the fact that there was a legal difference between town and country people. There is no doubt that the colonisation by the Anglo-Normans linked Ireland culturally and economically to contemporary developments in the rest of Europe.

Although Dublin is not included in this book I must mention it because it is the prime example in Ireland of a Viking stronghold which developed into a fully-fledged Anglo-Norman borough. Also, there is an excellent scale model of the late-medieval town on display in 'Dublinia', at Christ Church. This gives us an idea what a walled town looked like. The historical events happened like this. After the Anglo-Normans came to Ireland the English king Henry II promoted the former Viking towns. Dublin was the first one to be granted a charter, modelled on the law of Bristol, in 1171. In 1192 a second charter, confirming the first one, was issued for Dublin and this one set the stage for the development of an urban network in Ireland as it was also established on the continent at the same time. Although there were approximately 270 places in medieval Ireland for which we have some kind of evidence for the existence of burgesses only fifty-six of those are known to have been genuine towns from the functional point of view in contrast to the purely legal one. Looking at Ireland as a whole we see that the largest percentage of present-day towns have their origin in this period. The greatest density of these newly established medieval towns occurred in the east and the south-east, while the north-west which was largely outside Anglo-Norman influence was left out and had to wait until the Ulster plantation in the seventeenth century for the full development of its urban network.

In this volume we shall begin by looking at the small Anglo-Norman towns, Kells and Downpatrick, that were founded on the sites of earlier Christian monasteries. They show physical evidence of that early period in the present layout of their streets and the surviving monuments. No doubt, Downpatrick is the more imposing one, where the Anglo-Norman town developed in the shadow of the Cathedral Hill. The manner in which the large Gothic Anglo-Norman cathedral has replaced any traces of the earlier monastery associated with a slim round tower is a vivid expression of continuity of site and function but also of the change of material culture and the transfer of power which occurred after the arrival of the Anglo-Normans. The Normans liked to build big, as is demonstrated by the size of their cathedrals and their castles.

A large number of Anglo-Norman towns were completely newly built. Some of those were established in the context of a 'feudal' castle as the examples of Carrickfergus and Athlone illustrate very well. In both places the castle still dominates the present-day town. Both towns once had enclosing walls and they have a linear street-pattern typical of many of the planned Anglo-Norman towns. Sligo and Dungarvan, more medieval towns in our volume, are good examples of medieval towns without the presence of an imposing castle. Their main medieval streets were wide enough to accommodate the market.

Typically there was only one medieval parish church. But, just outside the medieval walls stood the Dominican and Franciscan religious houses symbolising the importance of the church. The Augustinian canons are the only large order whose houses occur more frequently within towns than without. The location of the medieval abbeys and friaries on the edge of medieval towns is probably related to their attempt to be independent of the jurisdiction of the town and to the likelihood that by the time of their foundation land within the walls had become scarce and finally to the fact that many of them served as hospitals for the sick.

In the political uncertainty of the post-medieval period towns in Ireland stagnated, but in the sixteenth century this situation changed, when the English government decided to reconquer Ireland by means of plantation. The Munster plantation in the late sixteenth century led to far-reaching settlements in the province and to the foundation of new towns by a few private individuals, for example Sir Richard Boyle who founded Bandon, which is included in our volume. Bandon had become a Protestant stronghold with neatly laid out streets and Protestant churches in prominent positions. A good example of a plantation town in Leinster is Enniscorthy, which came to play an important role in national politics. A long way further north the town of Lurgan illustrates the impact of the Ulster plantation.

Characteristic of towns in eighteenth-century Ireland is the intervention by landowners either by improving existing towns or creating entirely new ones. A recent estimate carried out by Brian Graham and Lindsay Proudfoot suggests that over 750 provincial towns and villages of all sizes throughout Ireland display some evidence of landlord impact. Our examples of town formation influenced by enterprising local landlords are Castlecomer and Ennistymon. A good example of a regularly planned estate town, included in our volume, is Maynooth, built by the earls of Kildare. The Irish landlords did no more than follow their English and continental counterparts when they introduced the concept of formalism into their settlements. But the fact that generally, although not in the case of Maynooth, they were the descendants of a colonial elite belonging to the established Protestant church rather than to the Catholic faith of the majority brought latent cultural and political tension.

One of the striking features of nineteenth-century Irish towns is the manifestation of the re-emergence of Catholicism as a formal institutional force. Contrary to the perceived image, institutional Catholicism was strongest in the richer areas of Ireland in the south-east, among the upper classes and in the towns. The building of neo-Gothic Catholic cathedrals in dominant positions and the religious houses of the indigenous teaching orders of the Presentation and Mercy nuns and the Christian Brothers, together with boarding colleges, created the new Catholic institutional sector on the periphery of the existing towns, as the example of Mullingar demonstrates so clearly.

Bray is one of the few new towns which were built in Ireland in the nineteenth century as railway towns or resort towns. Bray on the railway line from Dublin to the south and as gate-way to Wicklow happily combined both functions.

And what will later generations identify as the contribution of our century to the formation of towns? Suburbs and supermarkets, while the hearts of our cities deteriorate? The smaller Irish towns with less investment power have escaped more nearly intact than the bigger ones. But even there the last ten years have seen a change. The urban renewal tax-incentives have geared private developers into the city centres and government ministers now openly speak of the need for urban conservation. The promotion of heritage towns by Bord Fáilte has focused the mind on the past of many small towns and the publication of the *Irish Historic Towns Atlas* by the Royal Irish Academy provides detailed historical research on Irish towns in text and maps and is a contribution to making towns a better-known part of Irish history.

The topographical history of our towns as expressed in their streets and buildings can no more be separated from the history of urban society than one can separate the physical appearance of a human being from his or her personality. The challenge of this little volume is essentially a geographical one – namely to grasp the spatial aspect (the layout of the town plan) and the time aspect (historical development) of our towns at once. This should allow us an insight into the nature of historical change. We have seen that our towns reflect the culture of the coloniser and the colonised, but they also represent a unity which is the result of their own lived experience, embracing cultural continuity, cultural adaptations and innovations. It is in the concept of continuity within discontinuity, a pattern created by repeated colonisation movements, that the complexities of Irish cultural identity are best explained.

**Select bibliography**
P. Shaffrey: *The Irish Town*, Dublin, 1975
R. Butlin, ed.: *The Development of the Irish Town*, London, 1977
A. Simms: 'Cartographic representation of diachronic analysis: the example of the origin of Irish towns', in A. R. H. Baker and M. Billinge (eds), *Period and Place: Research Methods in Historical Geography*, Cambridge, 1982, pp. 289-300
B. J. Graham and L. J. Proudfoot, (eds): *An Historical Geography of Ireland*, London, 1993
*Irish Historic Towns Atlas:* editors J. H. Andrews, A. Simms, H. B. Clarke, cartographic editor K. M. Davies, no. 1 *Kildare* by J. H. Andrews (1986), no. 2 *Carrickfergus* by P. Robinson (1986), no. 3 *Bandon* by P. O'Flanagan (1988), no. 4 *Kells* by A. Simms with K. Simms (1990), no. 5 *Mullingar* by J. H. Andrews with K. M. Davies (1992), no. 6 *Athlone* by H. Murtagh (1994), Royal Irish Academy, Dublin

# KELLS

## *Anngret Simms*

KELLS is an excellent town for starting our series, because it shows that the origins of towns in Ireland go back to strong roots in the spiritual and economic life of the country. The majority of our towns date from the medieval period when the Anglo-Normans founded boroughs by granting town charters in a deliberate effort to strengthen their new colony. But a large number of these medieval new towns were not entirely new creations, because they were located either on the coast, where the Vikings had previously built up trading places, or inland where Early Christian monasteries had developed urban functions in an all-Irish-speaking environment before the arrival of the colonisers. Among those important early monastic sites were Armagh, Derry, Downpatrick, Cashel, Kells and Kildare.

It is Kells, Ceanannus Mór, in County Meath that we will discuss now. The town is built against rising ground, so that when we approach on the Dublin Road we make a gradual ascent until we arrive at the top of the town in a churchyard surrounded by substantial enclosing walls from the early eighteenth century. But the tall round tower and the four standing crosses tell us that the site is much older. Nearly a thousand years ago it was an Early Christian monastery dedicated to St Columba. In a twelfth-century description of the life of St Columba we learn that in the sixth century Columba went to Kells in order to meet the high-king Diarmait Mac Cerbaill and on that occasion Columba prophesied that Kells would one day be the most splendid of all the Columban foundations. And so it was to be.

When at the beginning of the ninth century the Viking raids made life unbearable for the Columban community on the island of Iona off the west coast of Scotland the monks accepted the donation of land in Kells and the abbot of Iona travelled to Kells and supervised the building of a new

*Kells from the south in 1820, by George Petrie (Thomas Cromwell,*
Excursions through Ireland*)*

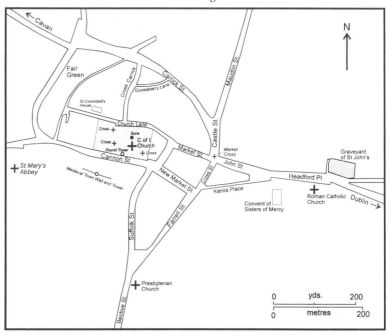

*Kells, based on Ordnance Survey of Ireland, 1:2500, 1908-11, and* Irish
Historic Towns Atlas, *1990*

monastery, which was in place by A. D. 807. A new church was completed shortly afterwards and the monastery flourished. Many people all over the world are familiar with the name of Kells, because the most precious relic of this Columban monastery is the superbly illuminated Latin gospel book known as the *Book of Kells*. This large vellum manuscript was kept in the parish church in Kells until 1654, when following a decision of the Cromwellian government in Ireland it was taken to Dublin and deposited in the library of Trinity College where it has been ever since.

For us this book has an added interest, because on blank pages at the back of the book charters dating to the eleventh and early twelfth centuries have been copied in Irish. They relate to grants of land and the purchase of land in Kells and it becomes quite obvious that the monastery was then a flourishing estate holding land all over Ireland. A large number of officials who are named in the charters administered the place and these included the head of the monastic school, the head of the guest house and the steward of the tenants on the monastic farm. A considerable number of people must have been employed in the monastery in education and in running the scriptorium, where important manuscripts were produced. Alongside these men of learning there were also the stone-masons who produced the magnificent high crosses at Kells and the silversmiths who produced the shrine of the psalter known as the Cathach of St Columba, now held in the National Museum in Dublin. These charters also refer to the *margad Cenanndsa*, the market of Kells, where cattle were sold. Before the coming of the Anglo-Normans, possibly under the influence of the Norse coastal settlements, these markets had become permanent institutions in the major monastic sites. We hear about the farming communities which developed within and around the circular enclosure of the monastery only indirectly from the *Annals*. They note that in A. D. 951 at least three thousand men were taken prisoner by the Dublin Vikings. These unfortunate people, inhabitants of Kells and visitors alike, were then marched away to be sold as slaves in Iceland or the Near East. These secular folk would have lived in wooden houses with thatched roofs which according to the *Annals* were frequently burnt down, accidentally or on purpose.

The wealth of the monastery must have been impressive. But given the fury of destruction is it reasonable for us to expect to find any traces of the Columban monastery in the fabric of the present-day town? We must assume that the site of the present Church of Ireland parish church of St Columba, at the top of the town, was the site of the original great stone church of the Columban monastery. Nothing is left of it or any subsequent Early Christian church building. But there is the round tower, the status symbol of early monasteries, standing 85 feet high on the south side of the churchyard. According to the *Annals* the tower, beautifully built of coursed limestone masonry, must date before the year 1076. When it was built it would have combined the functions of a belfry, a watch tower, a refuge and a treasury, where people kept valuables in time of danger. Between the church and the round tower we also find three elaborately carved high crosses and the base of a fourth, wonderful examples of the monastic stone-mason's craft. The oldest one, the South Cross, has been dated to the eighth century, the West Cross to the ninth and the East Cross to the twelfth century. When we look across the churchyard wall at the opposite side of the round tower we look down into Church Lane and there at the end of a row of friendly bungalows with chunky stone-work stands a well-preserved two-storey stone building with a high-pitched stone roof and only one small window. This extraordinary structure was built sometime in the eleventh century and it is possible that we have here the *diseart* or secluded place with its *lubgartan* or herb garden dedicated to Columba and mentioned in the contemporary Irish charter. Looking back into the churchyard we see a separately standing rectangular bell tower, the only remaining part of the late medieval parish church. Its spire was added by the first earl of Bective, the local landlord, in 1783. The present parish church, also with a slim spire, dates from the nineteenth century.

When we leave the churchyard we walk through present-day Market Street down hill until at a major street-junction we come across another very tall cross which before it got damaged stood at a height of about thirteen feet. It is a ringed cross with a particularly large base with figures of men and horses and an imposing presentation of Christ the King in the centre. It dates from the mid-ninth century. It is most likely that at first it was a termon cross, that is to say a boundary cross, marking the eastern exit from the outer enclosure of the former Columban monastery.

But we know that the cross also came to have a practical purpose. Pilgrims who came to Kells on particular saints' days gathered here to exchange goods. The site must have been the *margad* mentioned in the Irish charters and the cross became locally known as the Market Cross.

When we stand in front of the market cross we find that the streets leading around the top of the hill, Cross Street, Castle Street and Carrick Street, curve gently. In fact, they form part of a great arc which once constituted the outer enclosure of the Columban monastery. The inner enclosure around the core of the Columban monastery must have run more or less along the line of the present churchyard wall. We can easily identify this circular street pattern on air photographs and large-scale maps as may be seen in the recently published issues of the *Irish Historic Towns Atlas*. This type of near-circular street pattern also occurs in other Irish towns whose roots go back to an Early Christian monastic site, for example Armagh.

The street-names of Kells are an excellent guide to the history of the town. Let's go back to the market cross, the heart of the town. Looking north we see Castle Street with no castle in sight anywhere. But we know from the documents that the first Anglo-Norman lord of Meath, Hugh de Lacy, was attracted to Kells, probably because of the prosperity of the ecclesiastical settlement. Either he or his son provided Kells with borough status by granting a town charter. This was some time around 1200. This rather remote date is of great significance for the people of Kells today because the corporate lands granted to the townspeople on that occasion are the very same as those to the west and north of the town which the town council uses at present for the location of modern high-technology industries. But back to Hugh de Lacy's influence on the town in the twelfth century. His first castle was most likely a motte-and-bailey structure on the site of the later stone castle. The earliest cartographic record of any castle in Kells is on an estate map of 1762 belonging to the Headfort family who until fairly recently resided in nearby Headfort House. A watercolour of Kells dating from the period of the Napoleonic wars shows that the castle was a tower-house located opposite the market cross in the middle of Castle Street. By 1836 when the first six-inch ordnance survey maps were drawn the castle was already demolished leaving only the name Castle Street.

The medieval town charters stress the legal separateness of towns from their surrounding countryside. The physical expression of this legal separation was the town wall. What of the town walls of Kells? They certainly existed, because we have evidence that in 1326 money was granted to rebuild them. The only remaining section now stands at the end of the gardens of the properties south of Cannon Street. From the fields south-west of the town they look quite impressive as they are built on a sharp break of slope. The walls include one small round ruined watch tower which the local farmer uses for storage. We know from estate maps of 1813 that there were five street-gates. Characteristically Cannon Street narrows at the far end where the gate once stood. The roads coming in from Dublin and Trim, turning into John Street and Farrell Street respectively, each bifurcate just inside the spot where the former gate would have stood. Maudlin Street and Carrick Street also had gates which have vanished without trace.

Looking downhill from the market cross we see John Street. This street takes its name from the hospital of the crutched friars of St John the Baptist, which was located at the far end of the street, where we find the whitewashed walls of the churchyard of the former friary. Walter de Lacy founded this friary which suffered badly under the continuous late medieval border warfare which affected Kells. In the mid-sixteenth century at the time of the dissolution of the monasteries the church was the only building of the monastic complex which was still standing. Today only the raised churchyard is left. When you visit Kells do pay a visit to this churchyard and in the far corner you will have an unexpected encounter which will remind you of the medieval occupants of this site. On a horizontally placed medieval tombstone you will find the figure of a knight with a sword.

At the other end of the town we are in Cannon Street. No military associations, please. On the contrary, Cannon Street commemorates the fact that at the far end of the street outside the medieval town walls stood the Augustinian abbey of canons regular of St Mary, the successor to the Columban monastery when it was reformed even before the arrival of the Anglo-Normans. Hugh de Lacy re-founded the abbey and granted it so much land that it became one of the richest institutions in the country. The exact location of the monastery is open to speculation. The monastery suffered badly under the warfare along the borders of the Pale and by the time of the dissolution in 1539 the church buildings were already used as a granary. Today there are no traces left and only a public house in the general neighbourhood called Abbey House commemorates the name. At the far end of Castle Street, taking the road down to the bridge over the Blackwater, we enter Maudlin Street. In the medieval period a leper hospital stood outside the town at the far end of this street. Again, only the street-name remains of what must have been a great charitable institution in troubled times.

In any of the town-centre streets leading from the market cross we look at fine two-storey slated houses often with three or four windows on the first floor, fan-lights over the entrance doors and shop windows on the ground floor. These large building-plots are the result of amalgamating a number of smaller plots, which are still recorded in a valuation of the town in 1663. This was a bad year for Kells when after the confederate wars almost half of all holdings were recorded as waste or in ruins. In spite of its dilapidated state the town was granted in 1666 to Lt Col Richard Stephens as compensation for his participation in the Cromwellian wars. But perhaps because he could not face the task of rebuilding the town he very soon sold out to an English immigrant called Thomas Taylor, who was in possession of the town by 1706. The Taylor family was to become a dominant force in the town.

When we walk down John Street we come into Headfort Place, which is the street where the first three generations of Taylors lived. The name reminds us of the fact that in 1760 the head of the family was elevated to the Irish peerage as Baron Headfort, a translation of the Irish name for Kells. The name is derived from one of the Irish versions for Kells, *Cenlios*, meaning head fort. The name is still extant in the present street-name of Kenlis Place. When the Dublin physician Isaac Butler came to Kells in 1740 he saw Thomas Taylor's large dwelling on the left entering the town on the Dublin road. But in 1770 the Headfort family, like so many other landowning families in Ireland, left the town and moved into a mansion of their own, Headfort House, one mile north-east of Kells. This large Palladian mansion is now used as a boarding school.

Today the streets of Kells are clean and there are well-appointed granite kerbs at the street edges. But, as we know from the minutes of the town council from the late seventeenth and eighteenth centuries, this was not always so. Instead of cars people kept horses and donkeys which grazed within the lanes and produced dung, and the householders were fined for not removing it, such as the owner of a horse in 1705 'for annoying the streets with the dung of his horses'. The town council made a big effort to keep Kells clean and so they banned geese, ducks, pigs and pigsties from the streets. But there was a worse problem than dirt and that was the fear of the straw-thatched cabins without chimneys catching fire. To make matters worse furze stacks were kept behind the houses for firewood. A court of inquiry which sat in Kells in 1702 gave notice to twenty-two people that as a precaution 'they pull down their cabins by 15 April, remove their furze stacks by 30 April and that they begin to build their chimneys by 10 May 1702'. Such notifications were repeated frequently right through the eighteenth century.

When we look at the spacious tree-lined avenue of

Headfort Place with its substantial Georgian houses and formally laid-out gardens as they have survived beautifully behind the Headfort Hotel, we see the influence of the first earl of Bective who turned Kells into an attractive estate town. At the east end of Headfort Place he built a fine courthouse in classical style designed by Francis Johnston, which is still in use by the district court. And on the south side, right in the heart of the landlord quarter, he supported the construction of a Roman Catholic church. This fine late eighteenth-century building was replaced in the 1960s by a new structure.

On the far side of the medieval churchyard we come into a wide open space surrounded by houses. This used to be the fair green, created some time late in the eighteenth century. The whole raison d'être for Kells at that time was the marketing of the farm produce from the surrounding countryside. The Headfort family took their obligation towards the market seriously and by the beginning of the nineteenth century they had built a market house off a street which was then given the name New Market Street. Today some market functions are still held in the market yard which is surrounded by fine nineteenth-century stone buildings. At the lower end of New Market Street we turn into Farrell Street and we cannot help but wonder about the width of this street. The early nineteenth-century Headfort estate maps give the secret away. In an attempt to facilitate the passage of the mail coaches the turnpike trust had plans to run major roads right across the town through the medieval churchyard, which fortunately they never got round to doing. But they did succeed in straightening and widening Farrell Street. There is very little evidence of the first half of the nineteenth century in the fabric of the town today. It was a time when large numbers of hungry country people entered the town. In 1851 Kells had reached its demographic peak at 4,326 inhabitants. This number was halved by 1900. What happened? The traditional industries in Kells were brewing and tanning and they could not supply enough employment. The coming of the railways, still commemorated by a charming Victorian railway station at the far end of Bective Street, in some respects made the situation worse because consumer goods could now be supplied from a distance instead of being produced on the spot and breweries and tanneries closed down. There was not enough water for the development of any large-scale industry. Any employment in the old-established craft shops of for example shoemakers, tailors and carpenters or in the numerous retail shops remained within the established families of the town. The poor law commissioners gave a frightening picture of poverty within the town in 1836. Poor people lived in one-room cabins around little courts at the backs of the main streets. As late as 1891 the medical officer referred to houses in Bective Street as hovels unfit for human habitation. In order to ease the situation the town commissioners built several one- or two-storey local government houses in Maudlin Street, in Carrick Street and in Church Lane on sub-divided plots. All these houses still survive. The one-room thatched hovels in Gooseberry Lane were so poor that they were pulled down and the lane has no houses at all today. At the top of Gooseberry Lane in Cross Carrick we find a whole terrace of artisans' cottages which were built at the same time by private initiative. Their slate roofs, reflecting dark colours after a slight rainfall, are a delight to see.

Epidemics were rampant in the nineteenth century. Cholera broke out. The government set up a dispensary in Maudlin Street. A fever hospital was built on the west side of Fair Green in 1829 on the site where a big supermarket was built in 1981. A workhouse was erected outside the town, north-west of the Fair Green in 1840, which accommodated six hundred inmates. It was demolished in 1922 and has been replaced by a housing estate.

The religious and educational institutions of the nineteenth century have had a much longer-lasting impact. After Catholic emancipation in 1829 Headfort Place became the Catholic institutional sector giving a new flavour to the earlier ascendancy quarter. On the south side of this street next to the Catholic church we find the convent of the Sisters of Mercy who run a school for girls. The large nineteenth-century convent buildings still dominate the street. In the convent gardens there are two chapels of fine cut stone, one originally meant for the sisters and the other, removed from a deserted Church of Ireland church site, for their pupils. The boys were catered for by the Christian Brothers who built a school next to the convent. But before the turn of the century they moved into a fine Victorian building on the west side of Bective Street. In Bective Street they joined the Methodists who had built a simple church there and a manse. In Headfort Place we pass two buildings originally designed as banks in the late nineteenth century expressing some confidence in the commercial future of the town. One was the National Bank of Ireland, an imposing building which is now the town hall, and the other the Savings Bank built in an attractive Italianate style on the corner of John Street and Kenlis Place, now housing an insurance company.

In spite of the existence of real poverty at the periphery of the town there must have been considerable commercial recovery by the end of the nineteenth century because whole street-fronts were rebuilt at that time. Slated houses with roof-ridges parallel to the street stand side by side and provide a very unified impression. After the municipal reforms in the middle of the nineteenth century the town council worked hard to improve services in Kells. They fought a real battle against cess-pools overflowing into open ditches surrounding the town and against water pumps near leaking sewerage drains. A local government inquiry in 1877 stated that sewers were satisfactory in all streets except Bective Street and Fair Green. Finally in our century the sewage works were built north-east of the town.

A lot of effort went into supplying individual houses with water, which succeeded in the better-off streets in the centre before the turn of the century, long before it happened in the peripheral streets, where water pumps were used and where a corporation horse with a watering cart visited. The Kells water supply scheme was completed in 1897. The Kells gas works bought land east of Maudlin Street in 1859 and after 1860 they took over the lighting of the town. In 1877, so a local government inquiry tells us, forty-five gas lamps were lit in Kells every night. In 1878 the town council decided 'that a board be fixed in each street of the town with the name of the said street painted thereon'.

Visitors will still become aware of distinctly different quarters in the town, perpetuating the differences expressed in the mid-nineteenth-century tenement valuation. Headfort Place, John Street and Market Street with the adjoining Cross Street and Castle Street are still the institutional and commercial heart of the town, while the area around Fair Green on the whole provides more modest, partially public housing. A detailed population census of Kells in 1865 shows that the poorer areas of the town were associated with unemployed Catholics and the better-off ones with Protestants in the professions or trade. Today, with an ever dwindling Church of Ireland community the difference is purely income-related.

We can no longer find any traces of the Headfort family within the town. We know that after the famine in the mid-nineteenth century they progressively withdrew from the town by selling out leases. The decisions over the future of the town fell to the town commissioners, who by the end of the nineteenth century had changed from a Protestant to a Catholic oligarchy. Over the last few decades the town council has been successful in establishing high-technology industry attracted by the nodal location and historical setting of the town. On the Cavan Road we find computer factories built on former corporation land, a late beneficiary of the provisions in the medieval town charter, as we have already indicated. The increase in industrial development has led to an increase in housing, mainly in a private estate to the north-east of the town.

It is obvious from the busy commercial life in the streets of Kells and the large number of school children who come by bus every day into the town that Kells still fulfils central-place functions in the commercial and educational spheres. It is the seat of the circuit and district courts. The town contains six schools, of which Eureka, the secondary school on the Dublin Road run by the Sisters of Mercy, is the most impressive building.

The biggest problem for Kells at present appears to be

the threat to the fabric of the town from the heavy lorries which narrowly miss the precious market cross before they roar up the hill in Carrick Street on their way to the north-west. The building of a by-pass, as suggested by the urban district council, seems the only possible solution. The draft development plan for Kells also includes a preservation list which includes not only the ancient monuments but also a number of Georgian and Victorian houses. These are important if the centre of the town is to keep its old-world charm. But it is the heritage from the former Columban monastery which makes Kells unique. When we stand in front of the tall early medieval market cross or gaze up at the ancient round tower or marvel in front of St Columba's House or simply recognise the historical pattern in the alignment of the streets we realise that these are physical signs which provide the present community in the town with links to its distant past.

**Select bibliography**
A. Simms, with K. Simms: 'Kells', *Irish Historic Towns Atlas*, no. 4, Dublin, 1990
J. Bradley: 'The medieval towns of County Meath', *Riocht na Midhe*, viii (1988-9), pp. 30-49
A. Gwynn: 'Some notes on the history of the Book of Kells', *Irish Historical Studies*, ix (1954), pp. 131-61

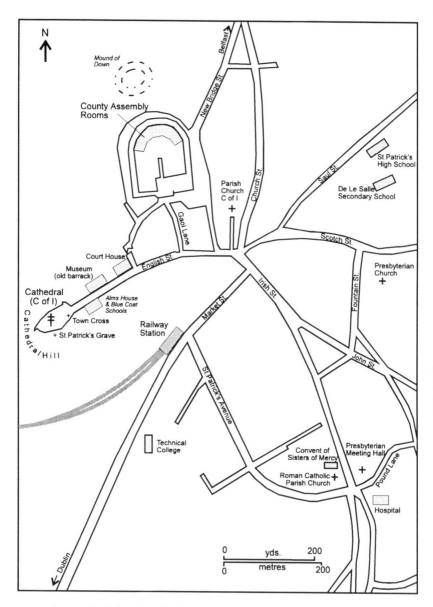

*Downpatrick, based on Ordnance Survey of Northern Ireland, six inches to one mile, 1920*

# DOWNPATRICK

## *R. H. Buchanan*

DOWNPATRICK, the county town of Down, lies some six miles inland from the coast of the Irish Sea, twenty miles south of the city of Belfast. The site of the town was described by a seventeenth-century visitor as 'built upon a beautiful hill, that rises gently from the innermost verge of Lake Cuan, which at high water forms a narrow bay at the foot of this slope'. Lake Cuan is now called Strangford Lough, and the narrow bay has become a broad expanse of marshland, following the building of a tidal barrage in the mid-eighteenth century. But the site of Downpatrick is beautiful still, the old town built on a low drumlin hill, and virtually an island in an inland sea, with newer buildings spreading up the slopes of the higher land that lies to the east and south. Westward across the marshes flow the gentle waters of the River Quoile, with the mountains of Mourne and Slieve Croob distant on the horizon.

The natural security offered by this insular setting explains why Downpatrick has been a focus for human settlement, at least since bronze age times. Its economic base lay in the waters of Lough Cuan – the bay most noted for its salmon fishing, according to Fr McCanna who came here in 1643; and more importantly, in the agriculture based on the fertile soils of the Lecale peninsula which forms its hinterland. Sir Thomas Cusack described this area in 1552 as 'a handsome plain and a champion country of ten miles long and five miles breadth without any wood growing thereon. The sea doth ebb and flow around that country so as in full waters no man may enter therein upon dry land but in one way which is less than two miles in length.' That one way lay by Downpatrick.

From early in the first millennium A. D. Downpatrick emerges as a local tribal centre, its present name combining the Down of early secular settlement with that of Patrick the

35

*Downpatrick, The Mall, 1863, by Thomas Semple (Down County Museum)*

patron saint. Traditionally Patrick's first church in Ireland was established nearby at Saul. But tradition also indicates that St Patrick was linked with an Early Christian monastery at present-day Downpatrick and that indeed the saint was buried here. The continuing political and ecclesiastical significance of the site certainly attracted the attention first of the Vikings and then the Anglo-Normans who came here at the end of the twelfth century. They came as warriors and stayed as colonists, recognising Downpatrick's strategic site and location in eastern Ulster as well as the economic potential of its surroundings. Over the next two centuries, Downpatrick developed as one of the chief boroughs of Anglo-Norman Ulster, along with Newry and Carrickfergus, surviving even the re-emergence of Irish political power in the fifteenth and sixteenth centuries, and the destruction of property and civil unrest inevitable in a contested borderland.

Not until the early eighteenth century did the town begin to grow again, its regeneration promoted by an energetic new landlord and his descendants, and sustained by the growing prosperity of agriculture in its hinterland. Walter Harris, whose *The Antient and Present State of the County of Down* was published in 1744, mentions with approval the recently rebuilt parish church and new alms houses, and notes: 'The town is adorned with several other handsome buildings; a diocesan school-house, a large market house, a horse barrack and a Presbyterian meeting house.'

As county town, Downpatrick developed further in the early nineteenth century as it acquired new administrative functions – the county jail and courthouse, a hospital and workhouse, and the cathedral which reopened for worship in 1818, nearly three centuries after it was burnt by the then lord deputy of Ireland, Lord Leonard Gray. By 1857 the Belfast and County Down Railway Company opened its line connecting Downpatrick with Belfast, but this new link to the outside world did not stimulate further growth: in fact between 1841 and 1901 population actually declined by one-third, from about 4,500 to just under 3,000. By the end of the century, a visitor described the town as 'until lately [a town of] considerable trade, but during the present century had steadily declined and its appearance now is distinctly dilapidated. Large houses stand unoccupied and stores and factories are falling into decay.' Part of the trouble was that there were few factories: unlike many northern towns, Downpatrick did not develop a linen industry and there was little employment outside agriculture, itself then in decline. The town lacked the economic base to develop a strong, separate identity, and some of its former business was now conducted through Belfast, only forty minutes away by rail.

Not until after the second world war did growth begin again, as the range of services provided by both central and local government increased and was administered in county towns such as Downpatrick. Health and welfare services, new schools and hospitals, and local offices for roads, planning and the agricultural advisory services all brought new jobs, both in administration and expanded retail provision.

In addition Downpatrick benefited from the new planning strategy of the 1960s which sought to curb the further growth of Belfast by encouraging development in specified towns. The planning strategy did little to stimulate new employment in Downpatrick, but it did lead to new public housing; and when sectarian troubles erupted in Belfast in the early 1970s, many families moved from Belfast to these new estates built on the town's southern outskirts. As a result Downpatrick's population nearly doubled between the two censuses of 1961 and 1981, from 4,235 in 1961 – lower than it had been immediately before the great famine in 1841 – to 8,245 in 1981. This rapid expansion has created problems for a town whose street pattern has altered little in more than a century. For besides the increased resident population, many school children are brought to Downpatrick's seven schools, and many workers in the health and government services commute by car from as far away as Belfast. At rush-hour the narrow streets of the town centre are clogged with slow-moving traffic; history is seen literally to inhibit the progress of modern life and there are renewed demands to remove old buildings, widen the streets and build ring roads to ease congestion. As yet these problems are unresolved, and planners continue to ponder how best to meet contemporary needs whilst conserving the fabric of one of Ulster's oldest towns.

Coming into the town today from Belfast, one is soon made aware of Downpatrick's long history, for the road is aligned on the tower of Downpatrick's Church of Ireland cathedral, visible high above the drumlins long before one catches sight of the rest of the town. That tower dominates most views of the city of Down, appropriately enough, for it is the site of the earliest settlement. The Belfast Road enters the town quite abruptly across the Quoile marshes, passing an estate of newish bungalows and a terrace of finely-proportioned new houses, built in vernacular style by the Northern Ireland Housing Executive a few years ago. In the past the Executive was criticised for some of its urban designs, but more recent work has been much more sensitive, and here and elsewhere the urban fabric has been enhanced by its new domestic buildings. Sadly, the Executive's own local office, built on a redevelopment site in Irish Street, is a different matter!

A few hundred yards along New Bridge Street, as the Belfast Road is called within the town, the dwellings of the 1980s give way quite quickly to a few houses built earlier in the century, and then to a handful of undistinguished public buildings – the telephone exchange, fire station, a few pubs and shops. The one exception is the parish church, a fine sixteenth-century building with rubble-stone grey walls and an unusual early Georgian Venetian east window. Before you realise it, you've reached the town's centre, a tightly-enclosed space where five streets meet – Scotch Street to the left, followed in clockwise order by Irish Street, Market Street, English Street and Church Street, the continuation of New Bridge Street from the town's northern entry. Most of the buildings here are no higher than three storeys – cottages which have grown skywards, retaining their domestic windows on the second and third floor, with shop-fronts at street level. This busy crossing place, the hub of the town, is dominated by one fine public building, the red-brick assembly rooms built by the town's landowners, the Dunleath family, in 1882. Its tall clock tower signals that this is the town's centre, the home now of the district council's art centre, with exhibition gallery and splendid small auditorium upstairs.

The odd thing is that the town's centre is less than half a mile from the suburbs on the Belfast Road, a very abrupt transition even in a town of only 8,000 people. There are two explanations. Firstly the present Belfast Road was opened as recently as the 1960s, and Church Street itself was only laid out in the last century: the really old streets in the town are the 'ethnic' streets, English, Scotch and Irish Streets, which date back to medieval times. The second reason is that this northern side of the town lies on the edge of the marshes, and historically, development spread along the higher ground towards the south-west, along Irish Street which was the road to Dublin. And in the long history of Downpatrick, Dublin was much more important than Belfast, the road to the south being Irish Street which thus carried the most traffic and attracted development along its length.

Seen from the air, or on a large-scale map, Downpatrick looks like a very large star-fish lying stranded on the edge of the Quoile marshes, its arms the five main streets we've already met at the town centre. We'll walk these in turn, and see what their buildings can tell us of the history of Downpatrick, beginning with Scotch Street. It has two branches: the minor road to the north-east leads to Saul, site of St Patrick's first church, and on to the village of Strangford, the little port at the mouth of the Lough whose name it bears. Until the present century, Saul Street was little more than a cabin suburb, a straggle of small houses and cottages. Today it is Downpatrick's main private suburb, a ribbon of development drawn country-ward by the presence of St Patrick's High School and the golf club – and the availability of land, relatively level and easier to develop than most of Downpatrick.

Scotch Street by contrast is much shorter, a steep climb uphill to the east of the town centre. This is the least pretentious of the town's three medieval streets – unpretentious I think, because it led nowhere in particular, except to the Gallows Hill where a gibbet stood on a rocky outcrop in full view of the town below. At the head of Scotch Street stood the cavalry barracks, a fine seventeenth-century stone building which was demolished as late as the 1950s to make way for new housing. Today it would probably have been conserved and restored, an enhancement to what is otherwise a dull street of ordinary houses, the sort you can see in any town in Ireland.

From the vantage point of the Gallows Hill we can see the line of Irish Street, climbing steeply from the town centre, across the spur of the hill, and descending even more abruptly to the old tidal shoreline where the road to Dublin headed south-west, winding through the drumlin hills to Dundrum Bay. Until the end of the last century, Irish Street was one of Downpatrick's finest residential streets, gaining its status from the home of the Cromwells, which stood at the summit of the hill until the end of the seventeenth century. The Cromwells – no close relation of Oliver! – held the manor and town of Down throughout the seventeenth century, and were unusual among its grand landowners in having a house in the town and living in it for at least part of the year. This had not happened before. Prior to the dissolution of the monasteries under King Henry VIII, the manor of Down had belonged to the Benedictine abbey which stood on the Cathedral Hill: there was no powerful secular patron to promote its growth, like the Butlers in Kilkenny. The Cromwells were minor gentry, and although the Southwells who succeeded them, through marriage with the Cromwell heiress, were energetic and effective developers they never lived in Downpatrick; nor did their successors. For 'polite society', Downpatrick in the eighteenth century had to depend on the clergy of the established church, the lawyers and army officers, most of whom lived in English Street, under the shadow of the old cathedral, standing on the hill.

Irish Street may have lost its social status when the Cromwells left, and yet it retained a certain cachet which was later to be exploited by the new mercantile class who came to the fore as the town's trade expanded in the eighteenth century. Several of their houses survive still, one of the finest ironically now almost invisible behind a high security fence, for it is the town's police station. Recently, enhanced security precautions have required that the whole of the lower portion of Irish Street be closed to vehicular traffic – a blockage across the old Dublin Road whose symbolism has not gone unremarked by local wags! The closure of Irish Street to through traffic has not been good for business, but enough shops remain to show that lower Irish Street was formerly the town's retail centre, the place where street markets were held until the present century. Here too, in the Shambles, butchers had their stalls, one reason, perhaps, why more of the better-class houses clustered at the top of the hill, away from the dirt and smells of lower Irish Street. Sadly, many of these once fine houses are now demolished or in decay, for the middle class have moved to the modern suburbs of the Saul and Strangford roads. But one house at least has survived, splendidly restored to become the social centre of the town's Roman Catholic parish. It stands beside the convent of the Sisters of Mercy and St Patrick's Roman Catholic church, opened in 1870 and now in the process of enlargement. Its finely tapering Gothic spire acts as an architectural counterpoint to the square tower of the Protestant cathedral on its facing hill across the town – a juxtaposition of the two churches reminiscent of Armagh, St Patrick's other city.

The Irish Street junction with Pound Lane marked the town's limits until the middle of the last century. Here was built a Presbyterian meeting house in the early years of the eighteenth century, a simple T-plan church, now the home of the non-subscribing congregation, and probably the least altered of Downpatrick's older buildings. Here too, where a stream flowed down the hill, were located several of the town's small industries – a water-mill, a farmyard, and the pound for strayed animals. The town infirmary moved to a site here in 1834, and the original building still survives, surrounded by a motley range of newer structures of all shapes and sizes. As county town, Downpatrick attracted several similar facilities in the course of the nineteenth century, including the workhouse, now demolished, and a mental hospital, built in 1883. Now that Downpatrick is only half an hour by road from the major hospitals located in Belfast the future of its own facilities is being questioned. If any are closed the consequent loss of jobs will be a severe blow to an area heavily dependent on the service sector and with few alternative sources of employment. The effect would be most severe among families who live in the nearby housing estates off the Killough Road, to the east of the town. These were built in the 1960s and 1970s, on farmland that lay beyond the rim of the hills on Downpatrick's south-eastern side, mainly to house overspill population from Belfast. Their design is typical of that time, a mix of terrace and semi-detached houses and single-storey dwellings, set in acres of mown grass and parking lots with few trees to give a sense of enclosure and proportion. There is a church and primary school, but few shops: services are provided in the town, but that's a mile away, downhill. The estates here represent the biggest development in Downpatrick's history, yet they remain beyond the urban fringe, socially as well as geographically apart.

Market Street, the fourth of our main streets, runs southwest from the town centre, and was laid out across the marshes in 1846 to connect with a new road to Dublin; some of its buildings even today show how insecure are their foundations on the soft subsoil with leaning gables and out-of-plumb window frames. Market Street now really is Downpatrick's main street, busy with shoppers at the small retailers – no national chain-stores here: the town's population is too small to attract them, though there are two supermarkets, as well as several banks and the post office. The movement of retail business from the town centre to Market Street came in the 1860s when the Belfast and County Down Railway came to town, building its station on the flat land below the cathedral and drawing trade towards it. The railway closed more than thirty years ago, sufficiently long ago for a flourishing railway preservation society to have been founded, and to start rebuilding part of the former track! But if the original railway station has long since disappeared, this is still Downpatrick's main point for exit and entry, through the bus station and the town's main car park – a grey and monotonous expanse of tarmac, unrelieved by any attempt at design or planting. Downpatrick's main new public buildings built in the last twenty years are located at this end of town: the public library and government offices, the college of further education, the council's leisure centre and a purpose-built shopping precinct. Individually none of these buildings is architecturally distinguished: collectively they add nothing to the character of the town and are remarkably insensitive to its historic character.

That character is perhaps best expressed in English Street, the last of our five main streets and the one least altered: it retains most of its eighteenth- and early nineteenth-century town houses, though many are now used as offices rather than dwellings. Apart from a few shops, Denvir's Hotel is the only commercial premises; its date-stone 'John and Ann McGreevy, 1642' proclaims its seventeenth-century ancestry, as does a fine canopied stone fireplace revealed in the downstairs bar during recent renovations. Denvir's was the bus station of its day, the place from which the mail coach departed daily to Dublin and Belfast, bearing the town's more prominent citizens who lived in their elegant houses, close by. From the town centre, English Street runs due west, climbing uphill and curving gently to reveal an attractive succession of two- and three-storey houses, each with well-proportioned door-cases and fenestration. At the top of the hill the street broadens into the Mall, the old town's main public open space, flanked on the north by the courthouse, the old county jail – now splendidly restored to house the county museum; and an elegant pair of early nineteenth-century houses, the Judge's Lodgings. This is the Downpatrick of the old establishment, the place for military parades when the judges and the gentry came to town – their club, the Down Hunt, stands beside the courthouse, an unpretentious two-storey building with assembly rooms on the first floor.

Across the Mall from the courthouse and partly obscured from view by the raised carriageway, is Downpatrick's finest building, the Southwell Charity Schools and Almshouses, built in 1733. The building is a long rectangular block, built in brick with dressed stone quoins: it has a central gateway, topped by a cupola, with wings on either side ending in two school rooms, lit by high arched windows and projecting slightly from the main frontage. The building and the charity are worthy memorials to the Southwell family who owned the manor of Down from 1703 to 1832. They never lived in Downpatrick, but the earlier generation were energetic in promoting and financing urban development, and they employed good agents. Through their efforts Downpatrick moved from the squalor and urban decay of the seventeenth century to the prosperous market town it had become when the last Southwell – Baron de Clifford – died in 1832.

By then the cathedral had also been rebuilt from the ruins of the medieval abbey. Today it stands on rising ground at the west end of the Mall, its eastern gable framed by high beeches, above which its tower rises higher still. It's a picture of great peace and tranquillity, for the cathedral stands on its own hill, almost surrounded by the marshes, with the River Quoile flowing by, backed by the low drumlin hills. A Christian church has stood here at least from the sixth century, and possibly earlier, for tradition ascribes its foundations to St Patrick. Many centuries earlier, a hoard of gold ornaments was hidden on the Cathedral Hill, an indication perhaps of prehistoric settlement, and discovered by a local antiquarian, the late Arthur Pollock, while digging a grave in 1954. Certainly recent excavations show a thriving community here in Early Christian times, associated presumably with the monastery whose round tower survived until its removal at the cathedral's restoration in the 1790s. The same excavation revealed ample evidence of medieval occupation on this site, and there is every likelihood that this became the focus of the medieval town, the Benedictine abbey superseding the Irish monastery after the coming of the Anglo-Normans in 1177, and the secular town spreading downhill to the marsh at the foot of English Street. Here a wall was erected, separating the English quarter from Irish and Scotch Streets on the opposing hill.

Unfortunately there is little hard evidence about this formative period in the history of Downpatrick. It must have been an important secular as well as religious centre to attract the attention of John de Courcy, a powerful Anglo-Norman baron who made it the focal point of his northern expedition in 1177. He defeated the local king, ousted the Irish monks and replaced them with Benedictines from Chester, and erected a borough which endured despite the loss of its patron in 1204 and many subsequent vicissitudes. Despite its importance in Anglo-Norman Ulster, no major castle seems to have been built at Downpatrick to uphold the authority of the crown, no stone castle such as those built nearby at Dundrum and at Carrickfergus. The only possible site is the enigmatic Mound of Down, a drumlin in the marshes facing the Cathedral Hill, whose naturally steep slopes have been shaped to form a mound set within a pear-shaped banked enclosure. It appears to be a Norman castle, a motte and bailey, yet trial excavations in 1935 revealed scant trace of human occupation.

Today the cathedral on its hill, the line of English Street and its associated lanes and tenements are all that remains to show that this was once a medieval town, an Anglo-Norman borough grafted on to a monastic settlement dating back to the early days of Irish Christianity. Such settlements are not uncommon in eastern Ireland, but they are rare in Ulster where few towns are older than the seventeenth century. By then Downpatrick had already assumed the street form it has today, a small yet very urban settlement whose three main streets – English, Irish and Scotch Streets – met in a hollow enclosed between two hills. During the eighteenth and early nineteenth centuries the town prospered and grew, adding new streets and fine buildings, yet as a community it remained like a village, a place where everyone knew everyone else, and knew their business! This sense of community has weakened with the sudden growth of population of the last twenty years, and recent development has done nothing to enhance the town's historic urban structure. Fortunately official policy now favours conservation and regeneration, so St Patrick's historic city of Down will hopefully find a new future for its past as the twenty-first century opens a new millennium of its history.

**Select bibliography**
R. E. Parkinson: *Historical Sketch of the Cathedral of Down*, Downpatrick, 1904
E. M. Jope (ed.): *Archaeological Survey of County Down*, Belfast, 1966
R. E. Parkinson: *The City of Downe*, Belfast, 1927, reprinted Bangor, 1977
N. F. Brannon: 'Recent archaeological excavations in Downpatrick', *Lecale Miscellanea*, i (1983), pp. 27-9
N. Brannon: 'Cathedral Hill, Downpatrick, Co. Down', in A. Hamlin and C. Lynn (eds), *Pieces of the Past*, Belfast, 1988, pp. 61-4
C. Doherty: 'Monastic Towns in early medieval Ireland', in H. B. Clarke and A. Simms (eds), *The Comparative History of Urban Origins in Non-Roman Europe*, Oxford, 1984, pp. 45-76
L. M. Bitel: *Isle of the Saints*, Ithaca and London, 1990

# CARRICKFERGUS

## Philip Robinson

Most people's image of Carrickfergus is of a splendid Norman castle, built on a rock promontory on the northern shore of Belfast Lough. Even today, eight hundred years after the castle was built, it remains one of the most impressive landmarks on this part of the south Antrim coast.

In 1635, when the Ulster plantation was already well established, the town of Carrickfergus was visited by an Englishman, Sir William Brereton. In his journal he described for us a town then over four hundred years old, but still somewhat English in character:

> *Almost all the houses in this town were built castle-wise, so as though the Irish made spoil of and burnt the town, yet were they preserved unburned. This is but a pretty little town within the walls of a very small extent and capacity; the only grace of this town is the Lord Chichester's house ... Carrickfergus is governed by a mayor, sheriff, and aldermen, endowed with great privileges, and is the shire town ... It is reported of this town that they have been always loyal and faithful to the state of England.*

In the early seventeenth century the town was indeed English in character, at least inside the walls, but beyond the west gate a new suburb known as the Irish Quarter had been settled by Catholic Irish. As a counterbalance, along the coast beyond the East or Spittal Gate was the Scotch Quarter.

By the time of Brereton's visit to Carrickfergus in 1635, the town had enjoyed almost five hundred years as the largest and most influential town in Ulster. To think of Carrickfergus as an English town, or indeed as typically Irish or Scots, is to deny its cosmopolitan nature. Just as the castle sits on a rock thrust out into the sea, so the town projected itself as a key point of contact between the three kingdoms.

In a sense, the story of Carrickfergus must begin before the beginning. Certainly the town was founded by the Anglo-Normans, but despite an abundance of Early Chris-

47

*Carrickfergus, c. 1560 (British Library, Cotton Ms, Augustus I, ii, 42)
courtesy of Royal Irish Academy*

tian sites in the surrounding region, it seems that no earlier settlement existed where John de Courcy decided to build in the 1170s. What did he find? The most obvious feature was the large basaltic sill projecting out from the coast, with a freshwater well on top. Castle building, using stone and lime mortar, was literally a strong point of the Normans, so the site would have held few advantages for earlier builders. The name inherited by the Normans was Carrick- or Knock-Fergus, in English the rock of Fergus. This rock was the one associated in local tradition with Fergus Mór who is said to have colonised the west coast of Scotland from east Ulster about A. D. 500. There he established the sea-based Dalriadic kingdom that included some coastal parts of east Ulster. According to chroniclers, King Fergus was afflicted with a skin disease and returned in the year 531 to search for a cure from the well at Carrick. He was drowned when his galley was wrecked on the very rock that contained the well. The body of Fergus Mór was supposed to have been taken to Monkstown, five miles west of the rock, where his bones were exhibited as relics. Perhaps, in a negative way, this story testifies to the absence of any early church or religious house near the rock, and confirms the virgin nature of the site occupied by de Courcy.

In 1177, only eight years after the Anglo-Norman invasion of south-east Ireland, John de Courcy marched north into the coastal region of east Ulster. He built a massive keep at Carrickfergus soon after his arrival, and possibly by 1178. Of all the defensive sites developed by the Normans in Ulster, Carrickfergus had the largest garrison throughout the early medieval period. De Courcy was made justiciar of Ireland by Henry II in 1185. This meant leaving Ulster, but he returned soon after to establish himself as a feudal, semi-independent leader, even minting his own coins at Carrickfergus and Downpatrick. As well as the castle, de Courcy is believed to have built the nearby parish church of St Nicholas. Both structures must have been commenced before 1205, for in that year de Courcy was expelled. This crown-sanctioned eviction was put into effect by the followers of a rival Anglo-Norman lord, Hugh de Lacy, who

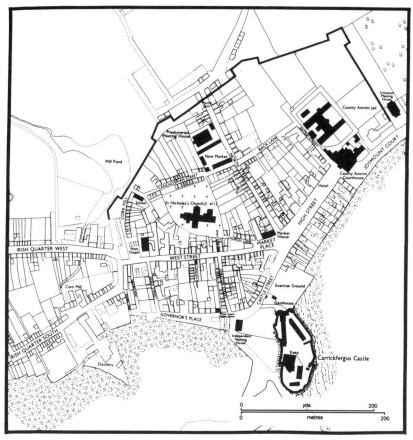

*Carrickfergus* c. *1840*, Irish Historic Towns Atlas, *1986*

was then created the first earl of Ulster. The castle passed
directly into the custody of the crown in 1210 when King
John came in person to Carrickfergus to take the earldom of
Ulster into his own hands. The castle remained, as it later
often was called, the king's castle, until 1227 when Hugh de
Lacy entered his second tenure as earl of Ulster. Finally in
1333, after the death of William de Burgh, fourth earl of
Ulster, the earldom (and with it the castle) became a crown
possession, as it has continued since. These early changes in
the control of the castle help us to understand the growth
and the layout of the early town, for de Courcy and de Lacy
each were responsible for the foundation of different

50

religious houses nearby.

An urban settlement in some form must have existed alongside the castle from the first decade of the thirteenth century. Burgesses were recorded in 1221 and Carrickfergus was described as a vill in 1226. According to tradition the town was created a borough by King John during his stay in 1210. It is difficult to be certain about the layout of the earliest town. St Nicholas's church had been built on a slight rise some two hundred yards north-west of the castle. A town map of the mid-sixteenth century shows a market cross at the west end of High Street, and this market place presumably occupied the open space between church and castle.

During Hugh de Lacy's second tenure of the earldom in the 1230s, a Franciscan friary was built at the eastern end of what is at present the High Street. So High Street itself may not have emerged as the central focus of the town until the mid-thirteenth century. By that time there were three important sites in the town: the castle, the parish church and the friary. High Street then connected the older focus of the town at the market cross to the friary site some two hundred yards to the east. In 1316, when Edward Bruce was laying siege to the town, a relieving force was recorded advancing through the principal street which was presumably High Street. The existence of a recognisable street pattern, such as is shown on the sixteenth-century maps of the town, suggests demarcated and organised property ownership. As was stated earlier, burgesses and presumably therefore burgage plots existed in the town in 1221. Burgage-like property divisions certainly existed north and south of High Street, and these can be traced back at least as far as the fourteenth century on the basis of recent archaeological evidence.

In the medieval period, an attack on the Anglo-Irish colony at Carrickfergus could be met by three lines of resistance. The hinterland, that is the county of Carrickfergus, was protected by a defensive line of tower-houses and forts. Within this the town was surrounded by earthen ditches and, as a last resort, the castle with its keep and curtain walls could be defended. The construction of the first town defences or ditches probably took place in the thirteenth century.

With the virtual collapse of the earldom of Ulster after 1333, Carrickfergus became increasingly under threat from both Scots and Irish. The town was burnt by the Scots in 1386 and a request to build and repair it the following year may have resulted either from this attack or from that of Niall O'Neill in 1384. The Scots again were the predators when the townsmen claimed that the town had been totally burnt by their enemies in 1402. Meanwhile an important branch of the Tyrone O'Neills had begun to move eastward across the River Bann, establishing their authority over the southern half of County Antrim, except for Carrickfergus and its immediate surroundings, as well as most of north Down. This was not just a temporary set-back for the Anglo-Irish colony, for the entire area occupied by the Clandeboye O'Neills was to remain the principality of these O'Neills until the early seventeenth century. The links between Carrickfergus and other areas under English law on the east coast such as Downpatrick and the Lecale area in south Down, and the Pale itself, could now be maintained only by sea.

Despite the strengthening of the outer defences of the county, the town was burnt by the Scots in 1513 and again in 1573 and 1575.

As far as Carrickfergus was concerned, the town which had once been the centre for control of a large earldom now had its bailiwick confined to a radius of about four miles. The exact limits of the county or liberties of the town of Carrickfergus are not known until the early seventeenth century, when the lands anciently belonging to the corporation were described in the town's charters of 1601 and 1609.

In 1460 the colony reportedly could coexist with the Clandeboye O'Neills only by paying them 'black rent' for protection. In spite of this burden, not to mention periodic destruction by fire, the archaeological finds in the town dating from the thirteenth to the fifteenth centuries reflect a considerable richness of urban life. The role of the town as a major trading post throughout this period has been confirmed by extensive and various finds of imported pottery.

The late sixteenth and early seventeenth centuries were a period of radical change for Carrickfergus. The town received a new charter in 1569 and there were several Elizabethan schemes for planting English colonies in its vicinity. The most important was that of the earl of Essex, who hoped in 1575 to colonise the south and east of Antrim, excluding of course Carrickfergus, which by its new charter was not in the queen's gift. However within a few years Essex and most of his followers were living in the town. The English adventurers of this period were few in number compared with the plantation settlers of the following reign, but it was with surprisingly little conflict that these newcomers gained the ascendancy over the old English or Anglo-Irish. Several families claiming to have accompanied de Courcy to Carrickfergus are named as residents in 1567, and were still among the leading families at the end of the century.

Tower-houses appear on all sixteenth-century maps of the town. One of these in High Street has been dated by excavation to the 1560s and another in Cheston Street to the mid-sixteenth century. Presumably the more archaic house-types shown alongside the tower-houses in the sixteenth century maps reveal something of the nature of older dwellings in the town. These were mostly constructed of impermanent materials during the medieval period. The municipal records state that in 1593 the houses in West Street were beginning to be built with lime and stone, so that the street was made 'fair and strong, where before the most part thereof was in rotten and ruinous clay houses'. Meanwhile, with a renewed charter and revitalised corporation, measures had been taken to strengthen the town's defences. In 1536, repairs had been carried out on the town walls and two maps drawn thirty years later reveal something of their alignment and construction. By 1567 the former Franciscan friary was enclosed by the same sort of earthen bank that surrounded the rest of the town. The earl of Essex was criticised by the then lord deputy, Sir Henry Sidney, in 1575 for not having properly walled the town with stone. In 1581 men were still working on the wall and by 1600 the sea wall had been completed east and west of the castle.

The first decade of the seventeenth century witnessed the arrival of Sir Arthur Chichester as governor of Carrickfergus castle. His two most significant developments in the town were the replanning and completion of the town wall, and the construction of Joymount House on the friary site. A new town wall, nearly nine hundred yards long, which included six new flankers and incorporated most of the sea wall previously completed, was begun about 1609. Evidently it had been completed by 1615, when arrangements were made to disband the workforce. The area enclosed by the sixteenth-century ditches was virtually doubled by Chichester's new wall, and what had been the old rampart along the northern edge of the town now formed Church Lane and Back Lane within the new extent of the town. It would appear from corporation leases of land in this area that the new intake to the north had not been previously developed. Indeed certain leases of land north of Back Lane referred to this area as the old bowling green.

Only after 1600 were stone and slated houses built in West Street and North Street, giving these areas distinct street lines which have been maintained until today. Within the core of the older town, the character of many of the buildings changed also. Stone houses, rather different in form from tower-houses, were being built. Despite being known as castles, these were less defensive in character. They had larger windows, were lower in height and had longer frontages. The castles, like the tower-houses, were concentrated along High Street, Market Place, Cheston Street and Castle Street. But new public buildings were also required for the new plantation order. When the charter for the town was regranted by James I in 1609, land was set aside for the construction of a new courthouse and jail for County Antrim at the west end of High Street. This was completed soon afterwards, matching the courthouse and jail for the county of the town of Carrickfergus, which already operated at the other end of High Street. Beside the quay another old castle was repaired as the customs house. Following the dissolution, the Franciscan friary had been converted into a military barracks known as the Queen's Palace or Storehouse. Its site was then chosen by Sir Arthur Chichester for his new mansion house. He named this Joymount after Lord Deputy Mountjoy, and his house was completed about 1618. Joymount was described in the seventeenth century as 'a very stately house, or rather like a prince's palace'.

By Chichester's time Carrickfergus had changed dramatically from the medieval town of earlier centuries. Its dominant position was beginning to be challenged by other centres such as Newry, Coleraine and Belfast. Not only were these towns convenient entry points for colonists settling the interior of Ulster, but they were favourably located as ports through which the surplus of the plantation market economy could be exported. It was the expansion of Belfast that did most to diminish the relative importance of Carrickfergus. However it would be misleading to infer a state of rivalry between the two ports, for many of the leading developers of Belfast were also freemen of Carrickfergus, as this provided them with exemption from customs duties. The most obvious example of such an individual is Sir Arthur Chichester, the principal architect of the plantation, who while resident in Carrickfergus was a dominant force behind the development of the plantation town and castle of Belfast and built dwellings in both towns.

The vitality of both Carrickfergus and Belfast during the plantation period was represented by the growth of the towns, the construction of new public buildings and the changing character of domestic structures, as well as by the expanding commercial roles of both centres.

The first of Ulster's Presbyterian clergy was the Rev. Edward Brice, who settled about 1611 about six miles northeast of Carrickfergus, in an area already well settled by lowland Scots. Although the surroundings of the town were increasingly of Scottish character, Carrickfergus itself remained essentially English and in 1621 Chichester introduced an English independent Presbyterian clergyman, the Rev. Hubbard from London. Chichester's walls separated the English from the suburbs to which the Scots and the Irish were banished, according to local tradition, although we have no record of any exclusion order. To the west of the town, the Irish quarter in 1812 contained an old mass-house near the site of the present Roman Catholic church. To the east of the town the Scotch quarter, known as such by the middle of the seventeenth century, had supposedly been founded by a colony of Scottish fishermen. The Presbyterian churches in the Scotch quarter cannot be traced before the nineteenth century but Presbyterianism must have dominated the religious character of this part of the town from as early as the 1630s.

Carrickfergus was one of the few Ulster towns to escape the physical ravages of the 1641 rebellion. Indeed it was one of the chief places of refuge during the conflict, although some of the attacks on settlers occurred just outside the suburbs. It was the replacement of the English garrison by Scottish troops in the aftermath of the rebellion that was to have the main impact upon the town. By the mid-1640s the Scottish troops based at Carrickfergus appeared to have been more concerned with the covenanting cause of Presbyterianism in the province than with suppressing the Irish rebellion. In the following decade the town again became an English outpost in a hostile region of Scottish Presbyterianism and the castle was used to imprison Presbyterian clergy. Enforced harmony among the settlers did not re-emerge until the last decades of the seventeenth century, when they again, as in 1641, found themselves under threat of attack.

At the start of the war between James II and William of Orange, Carrickfergus was occupied by Irish Roman Catholics, whose allegiance was to James. When the duke of Schomberg arrived in Belfast Lough in 1689, at the head of a Williamite force, the Irish troops burnt the suburbs of Carrickfergus as they expected a siege, but Schomberg took the town within a week. The following year William III made his entry to Ireland through the port of Carrickfergus, riding along High Street to the acclamation of the people. This brief interlude gave common purpose to the planter population in Ulster, even if further anti-dissenter legislation was to rekindle English-Scottish antagonisms during the eighteenth century.

The population of the town appears approximately to have doubled during the eighteenth century. This, taken together with a considerable rebuild, suggests commercial expansion. It should be stated however that the growth in this period was modest in comparison with that of some other towns of east Ulster. While Carrickfergus did not stagnate, its commercial importance declined in relation to those centres closer to the heartland of Ulster's expanding linen industry. Nevertheless the town did retain a strategic position of national importance. It was attacked by French troops in 1760 and by American revolutionaries in 1778. In 1798, when the non-sectarian but here largely Scots Presbyterian United Irishmen had most of County Antrim in turmoil, Carrickfergus remained solidly behind the authorities. Many United Irishmen were held as prisoners in the town and on the outbreak of the rebellion, the military, with some town volunteers, marched to confront the rebels on the outskirts of the county of the town. According to the Carrickfergus historian, Samuel M'Skimin, who was aged twenty-one in 1798, not a single house was burnt in the county of the town during the rebellion.

The population of Carrickfergus doubled to almost 4,000 between the early eighteenth century and the outbreak of the great famine in 1845. In the 1830s, the population of the parish was estimated to be 16 per cent Church of Ireland, 11 per cent Roman Catholic and 73 per cent dissenter. Six nonconformist congregations built meeting houses in the town between 1810 and 1879. It is not known when the first postpenal Catholic church was built, but the present one was erected in 1826.

As the nineteenth century progressed, the personality of Carrickfergus changed dramatically. Commercial growth, industrial development, and the opening of the railway links to Belfast all set the town in a new light as far as the rural hinterland was concerned. The port towns of Ireland have traditionally been outward looking, indeed by definition they were channels for international communication.

The story of Carrickfergus is typical of many historic

Irish ports, for there is nothing unique about its history of cultural tension with the hinterland. The medieval history of Carrickfergus can be seen in terms of an English bridgehead in Ireland for the laws, customs, language, economy and people of Great Britain. However this role ended when Carrickfergus was eclipsed by other more rapidly expanding towns in Ulster. In many ways, it was because the seventeenth-century plantation had changed the rest of the province that the previous contrast between Carrickfergus and the Irish interior was neutralised. Its personality is no longer that of a garrison port, an English cultural enclave or a colonial city-state. Yet so far as the town's personality has been shaped by its history, the castle on Fergus's rock still stands to remind us of how much the image of the present town owes to its past.

**Select bibliography**
S. M'Skimin (ed. E. McCrum): *The History and Antiquities of the County of the Town of Carrickfergus*, 3rd edition, Belfast, 1909
G. Campbell and S. Crowther: *Ulster Architectural Heritage Society; Historic Buildings, Groups of Buildings, Areas of Architectural Importance in the Town of Carrickfergus*, Belfast, 1978
T. E. McNeill: *Carrickfergus Castle*, Belfast, 1981
P. Robinson: 'Carrickfergus', *Irish Historic Towns*, no. 2, Dublin, 1986
S. Speers: 'The imprint of the past: the divisions of Carrickfergus', *Carrickfergus and District Historical Journal*, ii (1986), pp. 29-37

# MAYNOOTH

## *Arnold Horner*

Mention the name Maynooth and most readers will probably think first of its famous college. St Patrick's College, founded in 1795, has been one of the cornerstones of the Catholic church in Ireland, and now fulfils a range of academic roles as seminary, pontifical university and recognised college of the National University of Ireland. Readers with an interest in earlier history will doubtless also think of Maynooth for its famous castle, the stronghold of the great earl of Kildare, Garret Mór FitzGerald, the most powerful man in Ireland during the late fifteenth and early sixteenth centuries. The ill-advised Silken Thomas may also come to mind, as may the siege of 1535, when gunpowder was used to breach the castle walls.

For others, the present may be of more immediate concern. Maynooth may be better known for its large livestock mart or as one of those north Kildare places through which commuters and longer-distance travellers must crawl en route from Dublin. College, castle and commuter are all elements in the story of Maynooth, but our focus will be mainly on other aspects: the development of the early village, the layout of its buildings and streets, and the far-reaching redevelopment of the second half of the eighteenth century. In particular, we will focus on the wide, tree-lined, straight main street. The lanes, which both parallel that main street and lead off it at right angles, are of interest too; they are narrower and shorter but also straight. On a large-scale map, the street plan of this central part of Maynooth is quite striking: it is a regular layout, planned about the axis of the main street, and markedly rectilinear at the north-east end but somewhat less regular at the south-west end nearest the ruins of the great castle.

For any student of urban history, such a street layout poses questions, in particular when and in what circum-

*Maynooth, from the east-north-east in 1965 (J. K. St Joseph, Cambridge University Collection)*

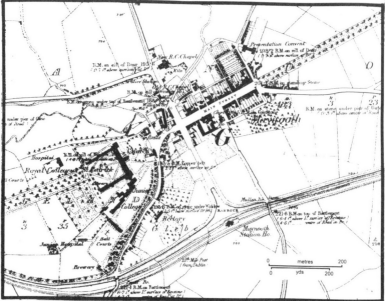

*Maynooth 1838, Ordnance Survey of Ireland, six inches to one mile, railway added c. 1846*

stances did such regularity develop and was a single individual responsible? Regular, planned street layouts occur in many parts of Europe. They developed at various periods and in response to various pressures. Some were associated with colonisation schemes such as the eastward spread of German settlers in medieval times. Others were inspired by the ideas of the renaissance and the desire to impose geometry on nature. In Ireland, planned street layouts are probably most readily associated with the eighteenth-century expansion of Dublin and Limerick, but there were also many initiatives in smaller towns and villages, for example at Birr (Co. Offaly), Bagenalstown (Co. Carlow), and Mitchelstown (Co. Cork). Other planned street layouts go back to earlier times: for example those of Coleraine and Londonderry date from the early seventeenth-century plantation period, whilst the near-rectilinear street plan of New Ross has its origins in the thirteenth century.

But our particular interest is Maynooth, and when and how its particular street-plan developed. We cannot fill in all the detail we might like, but, by drawing on material from three major sets of historical records, we can greatly amplify the more widely known historical facts about the castle and the college. The record sets we will use are (1) early maps, (2) the property lease memorials in the Registry of Deeds, Dublin – some of which go back to the early eighteenth century, and (3) the estate records of the landlords of Maynooth, that is the records of the earls of Kildare and dukes of Leinster, many of which are fortunately now preserved in the Public Record Office of Northern Ireland. Of these three types of documents, maps are of particular interest because they offer a visual record of changes in the street plan. With five maps of Maynooth made between 1750 and 1820, it is possible to follow the wide-ranging changes of this period in some detail. Surviving leases and estate records in turn amplify these maps with insights to developers, and to the length of the leases offered and the rents charged. Unfortunately, however, none of the records give us a direct insight on a matter of key interest: *who* re-planned Maynooth?

For periods before 1750, we must make do with a much

more irregular, patchy range of information. Nonetheless, to set the scene on our period of change we must make some attempt to explore earlier episodes, notably the medieval impact and the seventeenth century. In 1176, the district around Maynooth was granted to Maurice FitzGerald, an associate of Strongbow. Maurice FitzGerald erected a castle, and at some stage over the next few decades, a village developed. Whether this village was deliberately established or whether it developed gradually is not clear, but a chapel was in existence by the mid-thirteenth century, and in 1286 a patent was issued for a weekly market and a three-day annual fair; a mill was in existence by the early fourteenth century. Yet almost certainly the settlement was small; medieval Maynooth never appears to have acquired those trappings which distinguish towns from villages: there was never a charter, there are no references to burgesses, and no religious institutions such as monasteries or friaries located there.

The modest size of the village may have been in some contrast to the castle, and the contrast was probably all the greater as the power of the FitzGeralds, now earls of Kildare, expanded during the fifteenth century. The castle was rebuilt, a famous library was assembled, and in the early sixteenth century a short-lived college was founded. But this renaissance flourish was stifled in the 1530s, and it is not clear if there was any lasting impact on the village beyond the castle. Specific topographical detail really only begins to accumulate a century later. In the early 1630s, another great rebuilding of the castle was undertaken. Richard Boyle, the great earl of Cork, was one of the most powerful men in Ireland, and the guardian and father-in-law to the earl of Kildare. According to contemporary records, Boyle, who already had experience of castle building at Lismore, County Waterford, pulled down all the decayed old castle buildings at Maynooth. He then spent the then-very-large sum of over £2,000 in a rebuilding operation and in repairing the nearby church. The first known map record of part of Maynooth shows the results. The rebuilt castle comprised an inner court, with the older keep being flanked on three sides by new buildings, and an outer area with more defences and an extensive green. With an eye of faith, standing among the ruins today, we can perhaps picture the castle as the earl of Cork created it, with the balconies and cloisters of that inner court exemplifying the spirit of the late renaissance. Yet, like the magnificence of a century earlier, all this had a short life, for the castle was destroyed in 1647 during the conflicts that followed the great rebellion. It was never re-occupied.

But although the castle is now in ruin, there is other evidence of the continuing vitality of the adjacent village. Thus the Cromwellian Civil Survey of 1654 records the existence of two corn mills, one of them in repair, two small malt-houses, a chapel of ease, and 'two small bridges over two little brooks'. This information is amplified in some twenty leases surviving from the 1650s. From these, we learn, for example, that William Manwaringe agreed to spend £20 in building a 'handsome house of the English fashion, whited and glazed'. Thomas Symons, a tanner, also agreed to erect a similar English-style house, while Patrick Dunn, a gardener, was granted a lease stipulating that he develop 'a little spot of ground called the old haggard' and that he plant it with 'all the best sorts of ... apple, cherry, pear, plum, peach and apricock trees'.

Clauses in these and other leases show that during the late seventeenth century there was very considerable improvement to the surrounding countryside, with much new field enclosure and the planting of hedges and ash trees. We can perhaps picture Maynooth at the centre of this activity, its prosperity no doubt reinforced by its position on one of the main routes from Dublin and by a new grant of a weekly market and annual fair in 1678. At any rate, when the traveller John Dunton visited Maynooth in the 1690s, he was reasonably approving, writing of a 'tolerable village with one or two good inns where meat is well dressed, and good liquors be had'. But Dunton's comment is very much one made in passing. Neither from him nor from the legal documents do we get a more general sense of the appearance of the village and its layout. To get that more general overview, we have to wait for the maps made by John Noble and James

Keenan in 1750 and by the famous Anglo-French cartographer John Rocque in 1757.

These maps – and particularly Rocque's – were constructed to a high standard of detail. They show, and usually describe, almost every building and plot. So we can now locate the small number of public buildings, and identify other buildings such as dwellings, stables, and coach houses. Rocque's map shows some 120 dwellings, which may suggest that the village had a mid-eighteenth-century population of between 600 and 700. Eighty of the dwellings were described as 'cabins', forty were better class and described as 'dwelling houses'. The maps therefore allow us to estimate the size of the village and the quality of its housing, but it is at least as important that they tell us about the *arrangement* of buildings and plots. They quite dramatically portray a village layout quite different to that shown on ordnance survey maps eighty years later and so also quite different to that we know today.

What the maps of 1750 and 1757 show is that, with the exception of a straggle of housing along Parson Street to the south-west, almost all the village was located to the east of the old castle. A rather ill-defined axis was formed by the turnpike road from Dublin to the west of Ireland. It ran along what contemporary leases call 'the great street of Maynooth' before reaching a market place and then passing through the former castle yard en route for Kilcock. An overall impression is of a quite haphazard layout – a somewhat confused mixture of buildings, gardens, lanes, streets and open spaces, with route-ways widening and narrowing again over short distances. Most buildings displayed no regular orientation relative to one another. Only a few buildings had any industrial, public or commercial function. Industrial sites included the mill on its medieval site near the castle, a newly-built distillery in the castle yard, and at the east end of the village a bleach yard. As for public buildings, the only ones shown on the maps are the Kildare Arms inn on the north side of the main street, the newly-built charter school at the east end, the Protestant church near the castle, and the Roman Catholic chapel, occupying, as in many other Irish villages of the period, a less prominent position, in this instance behind the main street on its north side.

Although the village was not particularly extensive, the overall impression coming from these maps is of a settlement which grew over a long period in the absence of any organised framework. The castle, some streams and the route of the main road to the west, may have been broad determinants of how the village developed, but within this broad framework, individual buildings seem to have been added without any overall plan. Such a development pattern, which is characteristic of many villages in Ireland, stands in sharp contrast to the very deliberate reshaping initiated about 1750.

What happened about 1750 to stimulate what became a very comprehensive redevelopment? Basically, we have to take two things into account. First, the general artistic context. Fashionable thinking embodied an international dimension, taking on European ideas from the Enlightenment to promote new initiatives in art, architecture and planning. This was a period when improvement initiatives were espoused for their aesthetic, as well as for their potential economic, benefits. In some respects, the mid-eighteenth century was a bit like the present, with considerable interest in the quality of both townscape and landscape. As in the present, the local expression of that interest was uneven: some areas remained neglected, others greatly benefited from new initiatives. These initiatives did not come from the local community or the state, but from that contemporary figure of influence, the landlord.

In the case of Maynooth, the second element crucial to redevelopment was the arrival of an improvement-minded resident landlord. In 1739, the earl of Kildare, the descendant of the medieval owners of the castle, decided to develop the house at nearby Carton as his principal country residence. This project occupied the next decade, as did the creation of a greatly enlarged surrounding park. A great town house (now Leinster House in Kildare Street, Dublin) was also built. But by 1750 these schemes were either complete or well under way. It is easy to picture how, stimulated by progress on them, the young James, earl of Kildare, may have then decided to turn Maynooth into a village of a standard and appearance more in keeping with his own status and with the dictates of contemporary fashion.

In contrast to the earlier projects, however, the transformation of Maynooth was achieved only very gradually. One of the most important reasons for this was the landholding structure. Although the earl of Kildare was the landlord of almost the entire village, his power to make changes quickly was greatly limited by the fact that, in contrast to his activities around his own house at Carton, he did not have vacant possession. The village was in fact composed of over a dozen major property units, and most of these had been split further and sub-let by their lessors. Many of the earl's leases were for relatively long terms, and most had different and in some instances unpredictable expiry dates. With such a leasing pattern, the earl could make changes only by buying out leases, or perhaps by some inducement such as a land exchange. Alternatively, he had to wait until leases expired and he resumed direct control of a particular property. This, it seems, is the approach he mainly adopted, for attached to a map of 1781 is a note referring to 'part of the old town ... not yet out of lease'. Given these circumstances, it is perhaps not too surprising that it took some time to get the project under way and that it was difficult to maintain progress.

The first redevelopment took place about 1750 and was the north side of the main street at its east end. The map of 1750 shows a large vacant site beside the newly-built charter school, later the site of the Presentation convent. Seven years later, in 1757, Rocque's map shows part of this site occupied by a row of seven dwelling-houses. These are the slate-roofed, two-storey houses that today line the north side of that main street at the Carton end. Each of these houses fronted a rectangular plot 170 feet long, with most being 30 to 36 feet wide. Although by 1757 they had the appearance of a terrace, several different lessors, and by implication, several different developers were involved. This is one of the more deceptive aspects of the redevelopment process. Today, and notwithstanding many recent modifications, the main street of Maynooth *looks* at first sight a relatively uniform architectural composition: straight and wide, flanked by rows of two-storey housing. But on further inspection, minor variations in style and finish can be noticed between, and sometimes within, different rows of houses. As in the great Georgian developments of Dublin, there was a unity about the main planning framework, in the definition of streets and lanes to a uniform width, in the specification of plot sizes and, presumably, in building styles and standards. However, the plots were then made available, either individually or in small groups, as 'building lots' with leases, being offered to those persons willing to develop them; inevitably, different builders, often operating at different times, introduced their own minor variations.

Just as in Georgian Dublin, a street line could be laid out for some decades before even the majority of building-plots had been developed. The rate of progress was at least partly dependent on general economic circumstances, and whether developers could be found, but in Maynooth there was the added complication that, unlike Dublin where most of the Georgian development was on greenfield sites, the new town was a *re*-development, dependent also for its progress on such matters as when leases expired, and when older buildings could be cleared. As a result, phases of rapid change were interspersed by phases when seemingly very little happened. In general, however, the thirty years 1755-1785 brought major change, whereas progress was less dramatic thereafter. A map of 1773 shows that the east end had by then been completed, with nine houses on the north side of the main street, and twelve on the south side. Many of those on the south side had been built by, and leased to, a man called Peter Bere in the late 1750s and early 1760s. Bere seems to be one of the pivotal figures in the transformation of the village. His name appears in many leases, and he also seems at least partly responsible for the development of the lanes of slate-roofed, single-storey, labourers' cottages built behind the main street on its north side. Indeed one of these lanes, now Double Lane, is named as Bere Street in 1781.

In 1776, when the famous traveller and writer, Arthur Young, visited Maynooth the rebuilding works were clearly evident. Young commented on the regular layout of what he called the new town. He noted that, as the duke of Leinster gave encouragement to settling in it, 'consequently it increases'. Thomas Sherrard's map shows that five years later, in 1781, redevelopment had extended to about half the village. The main street is named Leinster Street and its line now extends to a bridge just before the castle. A market house and water pump are shown in a new square set off from the south side of the main street. Also on the south side is a new inn and ballroom, whilst, on the north side, to the west of Peter Bere's labourers' cottages, and still in an inconspicuous position away from the street, is a new Roman Catholic chapel. This building served as a place of worship until the present much larger church was built in the 1830s. The old chapel then became a national school.

I have concentrated on the early decades of Maynooth's transformation because, it seems to me, this period reveals quite a lot about the nature of the development processes involved. Later changes were of course also significant, and include further building along Leinster Street, the establishment of the college in 1795, and about the same year, the building of a canal harbour. A map of 1821 shows one other very important change, namely the re-routing of the road to the west. Henceforth, it turned before the castle and followed a new route, called Bridge Street, that ran past the mill. This new street was built about 1800. Some further changes occurred later, notably the building of Pound Lane in the 1820s, and the erection of more labourers' cottages, for example the now-demolished Dillons Row on the Dunboyne Road. But Bridge Street is in most respects the last major feature of the redevelopment programme which had commenced 250 yards to the east some fifty years earlier. Any further westward extension would have involved difficult changes to the castle and college areas. In any case a new main street was now in place, major improvements in housing quality had been made, and Maynooth now had a style and appearance more in keeping with its role as the village of the duke of Leinster. It now *looked* right, and it had acquired the architectural frame which it retains to the present.

There have been many changes in Maynooth during recent decades. Increasingly it has been affected by the spill-over of Dublin's growth. Many new housing estates have been added during the 1970s and 1980s. Over the last generation, the population has increased five-fold. The village has become a town of over six thousand inhabitants. As a result, main street Maynooth has had to adapt, and it has had to adapt too to the pressures of a heavy, near-continuous stream of long-distance traffic. Adaptation is evident in the transformation of houses to shops and offices, in wires, petrol pumps and lamp-posts, and in some inappropriate rebuilding. On the lanes behind the main street there has also been adaptation. Some infill of new housing has taken place, and many of the old labourers' cottages have been modified with the aid of home improvement grants. Some have become boutiques. Facades have been greatly altered, yet in some respects recent changes are just that: a veneer that is laid only lightly on an older framework. At some stage those seeking the story of main street Maynooth must focus on a fifty-year period of change two centuries ago. And, at the end of that main street, there are the great castle ruins, an insistent reminder that there is also an earlier history.

**Select bibliography**
[Lord W. FitzGerald]: 'Maynooth Castle', *Journal of the Royal Society of Antiquaries of Ireland*, xliv (1914), pp. 281-94
M. Cullen: *Maynooth: a Short Historical Guide*, Maynooth, 1979
Duke of Leinster: 'Maynooth Castle', *Journal of the Co. Kildare Archaeological Society*, i (1891-5), pp. 223-39
G. MacNiocaill (ed.): *Crown Surveys of Lands 1540-41 with the Kildare Rental begun in 1518*, Dublin, Irish Manuscripts Commission, 1992
G. MacNiocaill (ed.): *The Red Book of the Earls of Kildare*, Dublin, Irish Manuscripts Commission, 1964
M. T. MacSweeney: 'The parish of Maynooth', *Irish Ecclesiastical Record*, lv (1940), pp. 112-31, and lvi (1940), pp. 305-20, 412-28 and 497-509
Jeremiah Newman: *St Patrick's College Maynooth*, Dublin, 1984

B. J. Graham and L. J. Proudfoot: 'Urban improvement in provincial Ireland', *Irish Settlement Studies*, No. 4, Group for the Study of Irish Historic Settlement, Dublin, 1994

# ENNISCORTHY

## Kevin Whelan

IN Enniscorthy the locals will tell you that you are always at the top of a hill, the bottom of a hill, or going up and down a hill. It is appropriate, therefore, to begin one's analysis of the development of the town from the top of its most famous prominence – Vinegar Hill.

Transport yourself back four hundred years and imagine that you are once again looking over Enniscorthy. All round you now, stretching as far north and west as the eye can see, is a dense carpet of oak forest, covering the area between the Slaney and the Blackstairs Mountains. This was the medieval Duffry or Dubh-Thire – the black country, so called because it was black with oak. The fortunes of Enniscorthy are intimately tied to that forest and to the transition from a great oak fastness to its present-day framework of fields, fences and farm houses. Looking down again from our Vinegar Hill vantage point, we can see a boat-shaped island in the Slaney above the bridge. This is obviously the *inis* of Inis Coirthe, Coirthe being a Celtic personal name. Coirthe's significance eludes us, and the first historical personage we can trace in the town is St Senan whose church gives its name to Templeshannon, the suburb below us on the slopes of Vinegar Hill. At the centre of the modern houses, our eyes pick out a subtle but tell-tale feature – an enclosure containing a graveyard and a ruined medieval church. The enclosure alerts us to the presence here of Senan's Early Christian monastic site. Senan was a sixth-century saint and his establishment in a forest clearing on the river edge was surely a *diseart* – an eremitic contemplative centre. Templeshannon, then, was never anything so elaborate as a proto-town: it was a simple, small site, embedded in wilderness. Thus matters stood until the thirteenth century, and the advent of the Normans. The Normans, having entrenched themselves in south Wexford in the first years of their colonisation, began

*Enniscorthy, 1939-40, Ordnance Survey of Ireland, six inches to one mile*

gradually to probe northwards along the line of the Slaney, into what was still quintessentially the Gaelic country of Uí Cinnsealaigh controlled by the McMurrough Kavanaghs.

With an unerring eye for a strategic site, Philip de Prendergast, the Norman knight who was granted the Duffry, picked out a rock outcrop above the fording point on the Slaney. Here he built a small promontory castle as the centre of his manor. The castle performed a number of functions: it dominated the tidal limits of the Slaney and the fording point, it controlled the navigation and it protected the farming Normans further south against potentially disruptive attacks from the Gaelic chieftains. But the castle remained very much a military outpost: no medieval town grew up around it, and at best an anxious huddle of cabins developed in its vicinity in the medieval period. The situation was too exposed and tentative Tudor steps in asserting the hegemony of the central state were accelerated in the Elizabethan period. Government strategists saw clearly that the great surviving Irish territory in Wicklow and north Wexford was driving a dangerous wedge between the English-controlled areas of the Pale and south Wexford. Thus, Enniscorthy became an Elizabethan command and control centre from which a succession of tough military men like Nicholas Heron, Thomas Stukeley and Henry Wallop strove to subjugate Gaelic north Wexford. Henry Wallop was just the man to implement such a policy. In the 1580s, he gained control of Enniscorthy, which he described as the 'key to that broken border', and commenced a twenty-year campaign to push back the Gaels of north Wexford.

Wallop was a quintessential new English planter, a soldier, an administrator, a landowner and businessman. He was energetic, cruel, ruthless and competent. He utilised a potent mixture of force, legal astuteness, and entrepreneurial drive to break the back of Gaelic Wexford. His philosophy was uncomplicated: 'there is no way to daunt these people but by the edge of the sword and to plant better in their places.' His first move was to practically rebuild Enniscorthy castle for military use. His second was to exploit the great economic potential of the Duffry oak forests. This would eliminate the military advantages enjoyed by the Gaelic Irish in their woodland environment.

An additional incentive was that the cleared woodland could easily be converted into good farmland, on which an English plantation could be established. The woods themselves were also an economic source. In 1586, Wallop having been 'myself to view and consider the quantities and goodness of the woods which are marvellous great' knew that the Duffry was 'as full of as great store of ship planks and ship timber, pipe boards and barrel boards and all other kinds of cloven timber, strong, good and sound as any is to be found in any place of the world'. Developing the woodlands would

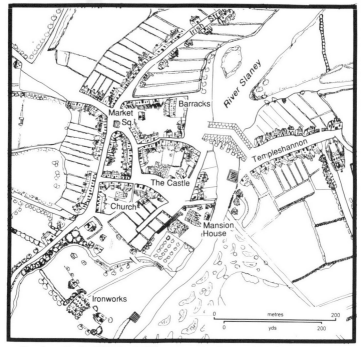

*Enniscorthy in 1729 by William Munday (Hampshire County Record Office). Redrawn by Stephen Hannon*

act as an economic sheet anchor for Wallop's settlement at Enniscorthy, which was ideally sited to take advantage of the timber trade.

Wallop built a large Elizabethan manor house for his personal use in the precinct of the former Franciscan friary. He got a grant of a market in 1586 and amongst other artificers drew over a number of 'timbermen and many cask board makers'. Thus the town of Enniscorthy was gradually accreting around the twin nuclei of castle and manor house with the economic lifeblood being supplied by the timber trade.

Spurred in part by Wallop's success, the Jacobean administration in Ireland embarked on an ambitious plantation scheme for north Wexford between 1611 and 1620. Newborough (Gorey) and Enniscorthy were created plantation towns. Like Gorey, Enniscorthy was probably enclosed with an earthen bank and palisade at this time; the names of

Duffry Gate and North Gate commemorate this episode. Within the earthen wall, typical long seventeenth-century burgess strips were created at the back of Irish Street, Guttle Street and Pie Lane and the bank apparently enclosed an elliptical crescent fronting the river.

The town itself attracted many newcomers: in 1617 the Franciscan Donat Mooney observed: 'Anglici haeretici totum oppidum inhabitant.' William Brereton, an English traveller, leaves us this vignette of Enniscorthy in 1635: 'The town is seated upon the fair river Slaney which ebbs and flows even to this town, the greatest part of all the wealthier inhabitants whereof are wood merchants.'

By 1641, the town could boast of many 'slated English-like houses well inhabited', three inns, two tanyards, a mill, a cooperage and a thriving timber industry. Across in Templeshannon, there was a cluster of thatched cabins. There was as yet no bridge, only a ferry – a long timber float set between two lines of stakes. A 1657 map of the barony of Scarawalsh confirms these documentary references. Enniscorthy is shown as an island of clearance abutting on the great oak woodlands to the north and west with a narrow clearance corridor stretching up the Slaney towards Bunclody. The castle, the mansion house and mills are clearly shown, as well as some large two-storeyed houses which stand in marked contrast to the cabin cluster at Templeshannon grouped around the parish church and the Jacobean great house of the Blundell family. The 1660 poll tax suggests a population of just over 1,000 of whom 16 per cent were ethnically English (Templeshannon was monolithically Irish).

The post-Cromwellian period was one of the most creative phases in Enniscorthy's history. A quirk of fate lay behind this. Robert Wallop, the town's owner, had been so closely associated with the regicides that he was flung into the Tower of London at the restoration. At this time, the English iron industry was beginning to have difficulties with its supply of charcoal, necessary to generate sufficient heat to smelt iron. Lured by the ecstatic description of untapped riches in north Wexford, and seizing the opportunity of acquiring a lease from the hapless Wallop, a London-based consortium was put together to develop an ingenious industrial enterprise. Their idea was to transport the ore and cinders necessary to make high quality iron to Ireland and to smelt it there in proximity to cheap charcoal supplies. They sent over Timothy Stampe as their chief agent and he chose Enniscorthy as the ideal site for the enterprise.

Enniscorthy had easy access to oak timber in huge quantities, a good river navigation and a pre-existing settlement under the nose of a military garrison. Stampe quickly set about leasing the necessary woodlands, building the ironworks and redeveloping the houses in Enniscorthy for the workmen. The consortium recruited the technicians and craftsmen with the necessary skills, seeking men 'bred in the iron-works' of the English west country. Soon, colliers, finers, hammermen, founders, carpenters, smiths and masons began to arrive in Enniscorthy. A furnace was erected on the edge of the town near the Slaney in the town parks, and subsidiary forges were built at Camolin and Monart to turn the pig iron from the furnace into bar iron.

The consortium, especially Robert Clayton and John Morris, had the necessary capital, entrepreneurial drive and commercial connections to make a success of the project. By 1661, they claimed to have invested a massive £30,000 in the Enniscorthy project and 'to have transported and settled there many hundreds of English to the great advantage of the English interest in this kingdom'. Enniscorthy, they argued, was now 'the hopefullest English plantation in Ireand'. The iron-works itself consisted of a furnace, a charcoal house, a charcoal yard piled high with cordwood, a lime kiln, a wharf and a founder's house. They were soon yielding a reasonable profit and the town of Enniscorthy entered a boom period. This was physically reflected by the building of an arched stone bridge in 1680 connecting Templeshannon with its thriving neighbour.

In the eighteenth century, with coal displacing charcoal as an operational fuel, Enniscorthy's iron-works went into a decline, struggling on with diminished production until 1792. The town now had to look to its purely agricultural hinterland to sustain its prosperity. The twice-weekly markets and the twelve annual cattle fairs were a help. In the wake of forest clearance, a vigorous tillage-based mixed farming evolved in the upper Slaney valley and Enniscorthy became the main marketing and processing centre for its products.

In 1729, we get our first chance to really see the town in a detailed estate map surveyed by William Munday for the earl of Portsmouth. Enniscorthy is shown as a compact, closely built-up town anchored on the crest of the hill. It is developed around the castle and bridge, and largely contained within a swastika of roads, running north (Irish Street), south (Guttle Street), east (Templeshannon) and west (Duffry Street). The Slaney frontage of the town was poorly developed in 1729, with only two small wharves, one at Templeshannon and one at the iron-works. This area was mostly occupied by the manor house, garden and orchard of the Wallops. Irish Street is shown as very well settled with its mass house discreetly tucked in at the end furthest away from the town. A series of lanes – Water Lane, Pie Lane, Blind Lane – are also shown. The castle is beginning its ignominious slide into picturesque decay, replaced by a foot barracks on the island strand. Templeshannon appears as the rather wide straggling street opening on to the bridge; its most imposing feature was Templeshannon House with its walled garden, orchard and grove. Based on the number of houses shown, Enniscorthy may have had a population of about 1,500, indicating a 50 per cent growth since 1660.

Half a century later, Lucas's *Directory* of 1778 and a detailed rental of 1785 provide another cross-section through the town. Of the principal merchants, two-thirds were Protestant, indicating that the town still maintained its earlier character. The most common businesses were grocer, publican and draper – comprising half of the total listed. A wide array of other shops was also present – four chandlers, four boot and shoe makers, two glass and china warehouses, two saddlers, a cabinet-maker, and an ironmonger. There was also a wide range of agri-businesses. Two clothiers and the sattinet and shag manufacturer, George Beale, represented the workshop-based woollen industry. This was especially evident on Vinegar Hill where Beale built forty houses with looms for his workmen. Two distilleries, two corn merchants, a miller and a maltster represented the burgeoning corn trade. In 1778, the town had not yet spilled down from its hilltop site, the town's merchants and shopkeepers still lived over their businesses and the hub of the town, both residentially and commercially, was the Market Street axis on the top of the hill. The 1785 Portmouth rental is extraordinarily detailed, listing every house, cabin and open space in the town. The most striking feature is the way in which the town was responding to the invigorating effect of the expanding tillage economy. The processing of agricultural produce was the primary function of Irish towns located in the lower reaches of navigable rivers in tillage country in the late eighteenth century. At Enniscorthy's fairs, the rental tells us, 'great quantities of cattle, sheep, hogs, malt, corn, leather and woollen goods, hats, shoes, etc. are disposed of'. Being so well situated for business, the surveyor believed that 'it will always be advisable for the present inhabitants to build good houses, shops, warehouses and malt-houses'. 520 houses are listed in Enniscorthy and Templeshannon, giving an estimated population of 2,500, a 60 per cent increase since 1729. There were now almost twice as many cabins as houses; in eighteenth-century parlance, cabin meant a small, mud-walled thatched house.

Two things were obvious about the cabins. Almost all had small potato gardens attached and they had been built by the town's merchants and shopkeepers, both to house their workforce and as speculations. In general, the town's cabins were infill items, squeezed in wherever a spot of land was free. A distinctive pattern was for a lane to run back from the street frontage along the length of an old burgess strip, which was then lined with cabins. Lanes, alleys, courtyards, approach roads, pieces of waste ground all teemed with cabins. The 1785 rental demonstrates the exhilarating impact of the corn boom on the town's economic life. It lists fifteen malt-houses, three drying kilns, two distilleries and a brewery. Other industrial activities included five tanyards, a salt and lime works, a woollen manufactory, a bleach green and a timber yard.

Enniscorthy thus evolved organically constrained only within the framework of individual leases. The principal tenants were the main decision-makers and town-builders in the second half of the eighteenth century, because the corporation and the landlord were virtually inactive.

The corn trade continued to boom. A 1789 advertisement described Enniscorthy as 'the granary of the kingdom for oats and barley' and frenzied investment continued in milling and malting. By 1796 the number of malt-houses had doubled to 29, of which 18 were held by Catholics. The mill mania had even reached the top of Vinegar Hill, where a quixotic windmill was projected, whose stump is now indelibly associated with the hill. The umbilical cord of the corn trade was the Slaney navigation to Wexford, carried mainly on gabbards or cots. At the end of the century, the great cataclysm of the 1798 insurrection burned over County Wexford and Enniscorthy was one of the main theatres of operation. Two bitter battles at the beginning and end of the campaign had a devastating effect on the town. A contemporary observer claimed that 478 houses and cabins were burned in the town, besides a great number of malt-houses and stores. 'It is an undoubted fact that the malt continued burning in some of the stores for four months after.'

In 1802, the earl of Portsmouth commissioned the local surveyor, Valentine Gill, to make a map of the town showing the damages. As a result, it was decided to build a totally new street, running directly from the Duffry Hill to the Market Square. New Street (now Wafer Street) was financed by the compensation. The Market Street-Back Street intersection was widened and a more commodious Market Square was created. Given the scale of the compensation, a considerable degree of rebuilding occurred, and the oldest surviving urban fabric of the town belongs mainly to this period. The basic architectural idiom was solid, three-storeyed houses, Georgian in style, with shops on the ground floor. In 1803 Edward Hay commented that 'the town is rebuilding very fast' and in 1815 Atkinson in his volume *The Irish*

*Tourist* observed: 'I perceived with pleasure since my observation of this place at the period of its misfortune the town arisen from its ashes in a style of superior splendour and improvement.'

In the first quarter of the nineteenth century, Enniscorthy's corn trade continued to blossom. In 1836, an estimated 36,000 tons of corn passed down the Slaney to Wexford, doubling the 1794 figure. Enniscorthy was now second only to Clonmel as an inland corn market. The town had a pronounced seasonal rhythm, with the great autumnal procession of slow carts creaking and clattering through its streets from as far away as south Wicklow. This corn trade finally elicited a major development project in the 1830s. Nicholas Ellis, agent to the trustees of the Portsmouth estates, developed what became known as the Abbey Square, by sweeping away the detritus of the old friary and the Elizabethan manor house. He also laid out two quays, costing £9,000, on either side of the Slaney, for the convenience of the cots. On this newly developed area along the line of the Mill Park Road, malt-houses, storehouses and warehouses were quickly built. Ellis described the results: 'the ground occupied by these streets and quays was taken from what were fields in 1822 and the stores and houses erected on those quays and new streets form a new town, lying between what was Enniscorthy and Templeshannon in 1822.' The Lett and Davis families were especially active in these developments.

The prosperous town continued to suck in people from its hinterland. The population doubled between 1785 and 1821 and by 1841 reached its all-time peak of seven thousand. This surge had two effects, making the town more Catholic in its composition and swelling the ranks of the poverty-stricken. Both effects soon showed in the townscape.

The Catholic church prefaced its institutional re-emergence in 1806 by seeking a more central location near the Duffry Gate for its new chapel. That re-emergence had a strikingly visible impact when Bishop Keating decided to rebuild that chapel in neo-Gothic style and to engage the great English architect, Augustus Welby Pugin, to design it.

St Aidan's cathedral was completed in 1848 at a cost of £8,000. The ravages of the famine meant that it was not then possible to add the spire. This was achieved in 1873 and gave the town its tallest building. It was a typical triumphalist gesture, signalling the church's pre-eminence on the skyline, as in daily life. By the end of the nineteenth century a distinctive Catholic institutional layer had been added to the town, with two cores, one at Templeshannon, and the other based on the cathedral complex.

But it was not just the Catholic church which engaged in a major nineteenth-century building programme. The growing social problems of the town, and the development of responses to them in an incipient welfare state, led to a series of public buildings. These included the courthouse in 1820, a fever hospital in 1829, a workhouse in 1842, and a lunatic asylum in 1867.

In the second half of the nineteenth century, the main development was the arrival of the railway in 1863 which killed the mail coach and stifled the river trade. The railway gave an industrial fillip to Templeshannon in the vicinity of the station. The Buttle Brothers' enterprises in milling and bacon-curing and the Star mineral water works were two of the most successful developments. Across the bridge, Lett and Davis's also benefited and made large investments to install the latest milling technology. The first Victorian photographs of the town capture the great cliff-like facades of their four- and five-storey red brick warehouses, alongside the cot-festooned quays.

By the end of the century, the newly nationalist ethos of the town was vividly expressed in the great centenary celebrations of the 1798 insurrection. The bicentenary committee then commissioned Oliver Sheppard to design a bronze statue. Sheppard promised 'to create the finest monument in Ireland'. His composition is a compelling sculptural statement. Almost simultaneously, P. J. McCall's anthem 'Boolavogue' popularised Enniscorthy and Vinegar Hill as nationalist symbols. The whirligig of time had indeed brought in its revenges. The croppies had come down from Vinegar Hill and were now inserted at the iconographic heart of the town whose initial function had been to crush them.

**Select bibliography**

P. H. Hore: *History of the Town and County of Wexford*, 6 vols, London, 1900-11

W. F. T. Butler: 'The plantation of Wexford', *Studies*, iv (1915), pp. 412-27

C. Dickson: *The Wexford Rising of 1798*, Tralee, 1955

P. N. O'Farrell: 'The urban hinterlands of New Ross and Enniscorthy', *Irish Geography*, v (1965), pp. 67-78

T. C. Barnard: 'The Enniscorthy ironworks', *Proceedings of the Royal Irish Academy*, lxxxv C (1985), pp. 101-44

# BANDON

## *Patrick O'Flanagan*

BANDON, Bandonbridge, Droichid na mBandon, is one of Munster's newest towns. With a population of nearly 10,000 people in 1821 it was the eighth largest town in Ireland, yet strangely, Bandon began its life as two separate self-contained towns in the early 1600s. One of these towns was called Bandon-bridge, the other, on the northern side of the River Bandon, was then known as Coolfada. In the early 1600s there were also two recognisable suburbs on the southern side of the town, namely Ballymodan and Irishtown or Cloghmacsimon. By 1618, however, all four segments of development were in the hands of Richard Boyle, earl of Cork, the most successful entrepreneur active in Ireland in the seventeenth century.

Bandon today, especially in its layout and morphology or structure, still exhibits the influence of its Munster plantation origins. It was intended to be a kind of early 'growth pole', acting as a catalyst to animate the plantation economy of south Munster. It was also designed as a military redoubt: hence its walls, although partly demolished in the late seventeenth century, have acted as a potent containing influence and directional force for subsequent urban development, especially street layout.

The visitor to modern Bandon is also impressed by the names on some of the shop-fronts, such as Herriot, which betoken the presence of the descendants of the original settlers who mainly came from south-western England. One of the earliest gravestones in nearby Kilbrogan cemetery indicates the resting place of Ann Dyke, from Bristol, virgin, aged twenty-nine.

The reconstruction of Bandon's heritage in the broadest sense is made possible by the fact that much documentation has survived. The tradition established by the earl of Cork in the management of his vast estate properties, industries

*Bandon from the east in 1775 by Bernard Scalé (Devonshire estate papers. Chatsworth House, Derbyshire)*

and investments in Ireland and England has led to the creation of a vast, range of material now available at Chatsworth, Derbyshire, the seat of the duke of Devonshire, whose family acquired much of Boyle's property in Ireland in the mid-eighteenth century. Other material is available at the National Library in Dublin and at Lismore, County Waterford, Boyle's Irish seat. This archive, which begins in the seventeenth century and extends up to the late 1800s, is one of Ireland's most important sources. It is for the historical geographer what Newgrange is for the archaeologist.

If one can mention ambience without being too daring, there is something in Bandon even today that makes it very different to most other southern Irish towns. Twelve per cent of its population is returned in the census as non-Roman-

*Bandon 1938, Ordnance Survey of Ireland, 1:2500*

85

Catholic. Admittedly this is a small percentage but when compared to the average southern figure of about two per cent it is significant. The ambience was certainly perceptible when I first visited Bandon in 1960 and it forcibly reminds one in many respects of what is now called Dún Laoghaire-Rathdown where I grew up.

Having disposed of our introductory remarks which have attempted to trace the origins of the town it will be most fruitful first to discuss the general morphology or structure of the settlement and then to examine the major functional changes over the last few hundred years and trace their morphological, cultural and social consequences.

Bandon consists essentially of two main streets, North and South Main Street, one on each side of the river. Each of these settlements was originally endowed with all the requisite paraphernalia for a seventeenth-century town. Each had a large gatehouse – part of the town's walled defences, a magnificent market-house-cum-courthouse, an Anglican church and a spacious main street whose houses had gardens stretching down to the river. All Bandon's major institutions and public buildings were located inside the town walls until after the mid-nineteenth century when a range of Catholic institutions including a church and a convent were built. Cabin suburbs appeared and disappeared on the outskirts of Bandon at various times. Among these was one called Sugar Lane which testifies to the fact that some of the early tenants partly paid their rents in quantities of sugar.

The completion of a series of military barracks, one in 1752 and two others at the end of the same century, made a significant contribution to the quality of the town's housing stock. They all served to prolong the lines of existing streets outside the walls of the town. Residences for officers were developed mainly on the north side of the town.

Industrialisation, especially in the late eighteenth and early nineteenth centuries, also brought considerable change: Old Chapel, otherwise Roundhill, developed on the outskirts of the town as a suburb. The development of four breweries and two distilleries at the same time also had important consequences especially in the eastern side of the town. Industry became a major employer and encouraged new residential development in that area. Finally the arrival of the railway in 1849, again on the eastern side of the town, helped to intensify housing, industry and street development there. Here on the outskirts of the town, on the hills overlooking the Bandon River, the town's native entrepreneurs built a series of imposing detached residences.

It would be fallacious to regard Bandon as an estate settlement. Up to recently its plantation origins have been the most pervasive influence. Although it remained in the Boyle estate and subsequently became part of the Devonshires' vast Irish patrimony, direct landlord involvement in the enhancement of the town, except during the formative period of the early seventeenth century, has been restrained.

The contribution of the duke of Devonshire was relatively insignificant by comparison with the major works he instigated and completed at Lismore and Dungarvan in County Waterford. At Bandon some municipal buildings such as the town hall were renovated by him or rebuilt. In the main his efforts were directed at enhancement rather than radical change. His most telling physical legacy was the erection of Bandon's most remarkable building: a striking fifteen-sided meat market or shambles on the northern side of the town. The rivers flowing through Bandon were embanked and transformed into attractive quays within the town.

To understand why Bandon succeeded when so many other plantation settlements failed and withered away in early seventeenth-century Munster it is necessary to view its early development in the context of the Munster plantation. The lands which were occupied became available for settlement in the period from the 1580s to 1650. They extended discontinuously from Dungarvan to north Kerry. Many areas were excluded, such as Cork city and the then thriving port of Kinsale. Hence, the new planters required a series of settlements which would stimulate the farming activities that were a central condition for the long-term success of the plantation. Bandon developed in this context as the plantation's pivotal settlement in mid-Cork. Other towns to grow up in this way were Mallow, Lismore, Newcastle West and Tallow. There was no overall plantation regional urban policy but rather a general desideratum that each of the major undertakers should develop one or several settlements. It was in this way that John Shipward and William Newce began building two separate settlements back to back at Bandon in the first decade of the seventeenth century. The early settlement of Bandon was one of a constellation of villages that sprang up in the middle Bandon valley such as Dunderrow, Kilbeg, Kilpatrick, Enniskeen, Crookstown, Castletown, Kinneigh and Newcestown. Some of the planters who came to Ireland were involved in a web of trading and exploration movements that linked south-west England, the south coast of Ireland, the Caribbean and east-coast Anglo-America. In this way Bandon's early trajectory must have served as a model of urban development in the early days of the English colonisation of the New World.

Bandon's leading activity, cloth-making, found no expression in the plan of the town. The cloth was made in the houses by men and women alike and sent to south-west England but principally through Kinsale to the Low Countries for finishing. The nature of this trade still remains to be investigated. The River Bandon powered a giant mill at Coolfadda which was built in 1620. It was one of two trundle mills to which most of Bandon's early tenants were obliged to provide corn and labour as part payment of their rents. Most of the farmers in Bandon's vicinity were obliged to discharge similar service. Early inventories indicate the range of craft workers employed in Bandon, among them bakers, blacksmiths, braziers, butchers, carpenters, cloth-makers, comb-makers, coopers, cutlers, dyers, felt-makers, metalmen, silversmiths, tanners, turners and weavers. This skilled group formed the most numerous element in the town's early population. The highest stratum was formed by merchants such as William Wiseman who built for himself an elaborate tower-house on South Main Street. Like several other resident merchants he exported cloth and corn while importing wine, sugar, spices, rice and tobacco. He also supplied, as an artificer, the resident garrison with most of its needs and was a considerable farmer. Servants and the Gaelic residents of the town, who mainly lived outside the walls at Irishtown, formed the lowest rung of the social ladder.

Still the economic vitality of early seventeenth-century Bandon depended upon the prosperity of agriculture in its vicinity. This was physically exemplified in Bandon's two elaborate market houses. Few farmers resided in the town but nearly all the residents had 'backsides' and gardens outside and within the walls which supplied food and apples for cider making. At this time Bandon exported semi-processed and unprocessed agricultural goods, especially butter, corn and meat, fish, pipe-staves, cloth and agricultural implements. We also know that it was a highly militaristic settlement. Besides its walls, its citadel and a resident garrison it had extra military capacity in that all its male residents were obliged to do military service as horsemen or footmen. Bandon also boasted three different kinds of prison. These institutions provide an interesting sidelight on early capitalism: they or the ground upon which they stood were rented by individuals on long leases to the corporation of Bandonbridge.

Documentary sources and early maps indicate the wide array of house-types which were built at Bandon. The leading gatehouses were the largest and most elaborate domestic residences, followed by sumptuous stone-built 'mansion houses'. There were also timber-framed two-storey gable-hearthed and hearth-lobby houses shown on plans which are datable to 1620. If these were the most common house-type in early Bandon they were larger and more solid structures than those built subsequently in the plantation settlements of Ulster. Cabins were especially frequent in Irish towns although they were not envisaged as an element in the town's housing stock.

Much of the credit for Bandon's early dynamism must go to its major patron and subsequent owner Richard Boyle. By 1622 it had a population of over 1,000 making it larger than any other contemporary plantation town in Ireland. By 1650 there were probably between 4,000 and 5,000 residents, a number undoubtedly swelled by refugees. In 1643 there were said to be 7,000 people in the town, all English Protestants.

The rebellion of 1641 ruined most of Munster's rural plantation. Bandon survived military assault but the town's vital support, namely a buoyant rural economy, was in shambles and so severe was the recession that many of Bandon's residents left for England and America. Yet in the early 1680s Richard Cox, a native of Bandon, described his birthplace in glowing terms. It was a town

> built within the memory of man ... fortified by eleven flankers and three of the stateliest gatehouses or castles in any one town in Europe. The rivers are so situated and the streets so placed that every house has a garden backward that reaches the river and the gardens being planted with trees in convenient places, in summer time this town seems to be built in a wood ... The inhabitants are all English and most mechanics who live by their labour which they do neatly.

Jacobite military activity towards the end of the decade that Cox wrote about was responsible for the partial destruction of the town walls and the total removal of the gatehouses, none of which were ever restored.

In the middle of the eighteenth century most of the town became part of the Devonshire estate, though the former Irishtown was incorporated into the Shannon estate, which belonged to another branch of the Boyle family. Fortunately for us, the Devonshires commissioned two major surveys of the town, one of which was an excellent map produced by one of Ireland's famous Anglo-French land surveyors, Bernard Scalé, which was finished in 1775. Scalé's map and terrier indicate that Bandon retained a population of 4,000 people but there had been few additions to the housing stock since the seventeenth century and little had been added to the ensemble of public buildings.

Significantly, however, analysis of Scalé's work reveals that important but subtle changes had taken place in the settlement's economic structures. In a word, diversification sums up the transformation. The northern side of the town had developed into an industrial suburb. Here there were over a score of tanyards, showing that the processing of agricultural goods was still a leading activity. The smell from these water-filled pits must have been unbearable for nearby residents whose houses abutted on to the yards. The presence in the same area of half a dozen brewhouses and malt-houses (where beer was both produced and sold) must have been a mitigating factor for some local residents at least.

The area delimited by the town walls remained the most salubrious part of the settlement. Here were located the most valuable and elaborate houses. Many of these had highly ornamented gardens, several of them possessing individual orchards. Slate-roofed, two-storey houses were typical: detached houses and cabins were rare. Many of these houses also boasted stables and offices, some of which were presumably workshops. It is also worth noting that Bandon never saw the emergence of a rentier element within the town. Unlike Youghal or Kinsale, towns with more ancient roots, it had few head leaseholders controlling more than half a dozen houses. The only exceptions were in the context of lowly cabin dwellings of little value on the town's outskirts.

On the leading approach roads into the town a range of house-types was apparent. By and large, thatched cabins were most frequent. Here labourers and servants resided, nearly all of whom were Roman Catholics. Evidence from the Registry of Deeds in Dublin reveals that on some of these roads a new Roman Catholic artisan class of bakers, maltsters, shoemakers, tanners and victuallers had crystallised, some of whom now lived in moderately large houses. This was a new departure, as hitherto people with surnames of Gaelic origin had been associated with the most menial activities and squalid housing conditions.

The centre of the settlement however, remained Protestant. Up to eighty per cent of the residents of the town's main streets are returned as such. We can be in no doubt that throughout most of the eighteenth century Bandon was residentially segregated to a high degree. This spatial segregation is also reflected in deep occupational, social and cultural cleavages about which only inferential evidence has survived.

Protestantism in Bandon was no monolith. Anglicanism was paramount, symbolised by its two magnificent churches. Methodism was very strong. There were also Quakers, Presbyterians, Primitive Methodists and Unitarians, each of whom had their own place of worship and often a school and meeting house as well.

Textile production remained a constant element, conducted by people using looms in their own houses. Before the nineteenth century this industry had little impact upon the fabric of the town. Camlets made from wool formed the most durable product: they were still exported to the continent. Linen production increased towards the end of the eighteenth century and cotton became important at the same time. All of these were initially produced within a 'cottage' context.

The early years of the nineteenth century witnessed profound and intensive changes in the physical, social and cultural morphology of the town. These departures were prompted by a distinctive if relatively ephemeral bout of industrial activity. Again, Bandon's development at this time was interesting. Local entrepreneurial flair and investment acted as the motor for this period of transformation. Landlord involvement was neutral, being confined, as we have seen, to embellishment. Most of the new plants were industries as we define them today. They were labour-intensive production units, largely dependent upon water power to drive their machines. Of these, George Allman's impressive cotton mill at Overton on Bandon's outskirts employed hundreds of skilled people. It was opened in the early 1800s but it closed before 1830. There were other mills at Castlenalact, Derrygarriffe and Old Chapel. To add to this suite of textile units of production there were within the town also another smaller cotton factory, a 'manufactory of fine stuffs', a corduroy factory and a woollen mill as well as several rope walks. An inventory of contemporary occupations reveals the persistence of the 'putting-out' tradition of textile production in many individual residences as revealed by the presence of many spinners and cord-winders as well as those concerned with ancillary activities such as button-makers and dyers.

The failure of the mill at Overton was precipitated by technological innovation in England and left hundreds jobless. A census of the Anglican parishioners conducted in the 1830s illustrates the consequences of this closure. Many are returned as 'gone to England or America'. Approximately 800 people left Bandon in the 1830s. Within a decade the number of weavers dropped from 2,000 to 30. Most ultimately settled and worked in textile activity in America and nearly all of those who went were Anglicans. The ruins of the enormous factory are set in the middle of green fields outside the town.

All was not lost. The Allmans invested in an elaborate distillery. It was erected on the eastern outskirts of the town and served to transform this previously weakly developed zone, much of the land being reclaimed from the river. With the arrival of the railway in the 1840s a further area of land outside Irishtown was given over to sidings and sheds. Finally, a gas works, Bandon's union workhouse and a large woollen manufactory colonised the newly created open space. Little residential development was however to transpire here except a row of houses built by the Allmans for some of their skilled workers.

In the mid-nineteenth century Bandon could boast of three distilleries and four breweries beside six flour and corn mills, two of which were of considerable size and all of which supplied raw materials to the liquor industries. By and large the bigger industries sought locations on the outskirts of the town to maximise accessibility. Watergate Street, earlier famous for a 'house of call' or brothel, pulled in a sizeable brewery and several tanneries as well, all attracted by the river.

The former walled area of the town which enclosed South Main Street and much of North Main Street recorded a wider mix of activities than heretofore. Residential properties were now interdigitated with retail outlets. Banks had become established on the Main Streets. The building of several new quays by the duke of Devonshire radically transformed the physical structure of the south side of the town. The south bank of the river was embanked and a road developed which linked this new quay called Burlington Quay to Weir Street and Bridge Street. Market Quay was constructed beside the newly embanked Bridewell River. Access to the back of South Main Street was facilitated and a range of small manufacturing units was established in the former 'backsides and gardens'. Among these can be noted factories which produced soaps, tobacco, coaches, dyes and mineral waters. The western approach roads into Bandon also witnessed considerable industrial development. Here some of the larger space-demanding industries were established: here, for example, on New Road, there was a brewery, a distillery, several flour mills and a large tanyard. The same pattern was repeated in the northern sector of the town. Several of the former tanyards had disappeared and had been replaced by fine town houses, many of which were occupied by officers of Bandon's three military barracks. This was the case along much of North Main Street.

Bandon reached its demographic spring tide in 1821 with a population of over 10,000. The rapid industrialisation of the settlement drew people to it like a magnet. The educational and religious demands of this large population saw nearly all the existing churches being either rebuilt or extensively modified such as St Peter's Anglican church. Bandon's first major Roman Catholic church, dedicated to St Patrick, was opened in 1861 and the Presentation sisters opened their convent in 1829. Still, no Roman Catholic institution is located within the former walled area.

The meteoric industrial growth of the town occasioned fundamental changes in the ethnic and religious composition of the population. Some time between 1796 and 1821 the Protestant majority was replaced by a Roman Catholic one. During the period in question the population increased from 4,600 to 10,000 people.

Bandon's idiosyncratic nineteenth-century historian, George Bennett, throws light upon the residential and wider cultural consequences of these changes. He wrote about the early years of the nineteenth century:

*It was about this time that the first Roman Catholic shopkeepers ventured to reside in any of our principal streets ... Previously some Roman Catholics had crept into the town, but they were content with the humblest habitations within the walls and in the most out-of-the-way places.*

The ambience of the town took longer to change. The travel writer A. B. Stark wrote in 1850: 'Bandon is in the main an English and Protestant town. Catholics there are in all parts of the place, but with few exceptions, they are hewers of wood and drawers of water.' Even by this time, people with surnames of Gaelic origin equalled those with surnames of English origin on the town's principal main streets.

Bandon's rapid industrialisation was followed by equally precipitate de-industrialisation. This decline persisted for more than a century as highlighted by a continuing demographic haemorrhage. Cotton manufacturing collapsed. This was soon followed by the closure of a distillery and two breweries. Local tradition asserts that a teetotal campaign was responsible for the demise of one such establishment. Some of the corn mills also failed and the last major tannery at East Gully also closed.

Bandon's population fell to a low of 2,005 in 1981 from its crest of 10,000 in 1821. In 1986 a population of 1,943 was recorded but here we are not simply dealing with a continuance of decline. Loss there was from the central zone but several new housing estates and many single houses were built outside the official boundaries of the settlement.

The continuing loss of so many manufacturing units during the nineteenth century was compensated, in part, by a growth in services and in trades brought about through enhanced accessibility conferred by the railway and improved roads. Bandon became the linchpin in overland communication between south-west Cork and the remainder of the county. The presence of at least a dozen pawn shops reflected the more painful side of trading expansion.

Decline too can have its benefits. This is the case in Bandon where most of the town's nineteenth-century fabric has survived to the present day. This has bequeathed to us an interesting ensemble of houses and public buildings of mainly early to middle nineteenth-century vintage besides many eighteenth-century houses.

While the later part of the nineteenth century like the mid-seventeenth century was a painful period for the town and its communities, the final years of the twentieth century have brought prosperity, dignity and confidence to many Bandonians. There is now a solid awareness that the heritage of the town, in all its aspects, is the property of today's residents which must be understood, treasured and conserved.

Bandon may have been passed over in the early days of rural industrialisation in the 1960s but today it counts several labour-intensive factories including one major multinational. It is the main mart for west Cork and the centre of a garda administrative zone. It has a range of retail and service functions which have captured an extensive hinterland. More broadly based than heretofore, Bandon's range of functions equips it to face the future with considerable confidence.

**Select bibliography**
G. Bennett: *The History of Bandon and the Principal Towns in the West Riding of County Cork*, Cork, 1869
M. MacCarthy-Morrogh: *The Munster Plantation, English Migration to Southern Ireland, 1583–1641*, Oxford, 1986
D. S. O'Donoghue: *Droichead na Banndan: a History of Bandon*, Cork, 1970
P. O'Flanagan: 'Bandon', *Irish Historic Towns Atlas*, no. 3, Dublin, 1988
P. O'Flanagan: 'Urban minorities and majorities: Catholics and Protestants in Munster towns c. 1659–1850', in W. J. Smyth and K. Whelan (eds), *Common Ground*, Cork, 1988, pp. 124-48
P. O'Flanagan: 'Bandon in the eighteenth century; the view from a terrier and a survey', *Bandon Historical Journal*, v (1989), pp. 49-57

# LURGAN

## W. H. Crawford

NOWADAYS Lurgan is considered a suburb of Craigavon, the new city created in north Armagh. Yet its long, broad main street would not disgrace many a larger city. Around the market place, however, the buildings have the scale of a provincial town. Their fronts have been subdivided too often and they are punctuated with archways. The southern half of the street is rather grander and more residential in character, away from the bustle of the market place. The side streets seem to be afterthoughts. It is easy to forget that Lurgan was itself once a new town established by British colonists in an under-developed region.

The town of Lurgan was founded in 1610 under the scheme for the plantation of Ulster. John Brownlow, an immigrant from Nottingham in England, chose the site for the chief town on the estate that he and his son, William, had acquired from the crown. The original name of the townland was Lurgyvallivackan – 'the townland of McCann on the ridge' – and it was the long ridge that gave the new town its name. The site was not central to the fourteen-square-mile estate but lay near its south-east corner safely above the fenlands that fringed the southern shores of Lough Neagh. The ridge ran in a south-easterly direction for half a mile and was separated on the east by a steep valley from another ridge on which was to be constructed the landlord's new castle and bawn. At its northern end the ridge broadened and sloped away in the direction of an old church which gave the name Shankill to the parish as well as the townland in which it lay. There the long, broad main street of the town widened further into an extensive triangular market place. The layout of the town contained no defensive provisions. In time of danger the townspeople could only retire to the castle: in 1622 William Brownlow told commissioners that he had in his castle shot and pikes for fifty men.

*Lurgan, Main Street and Shankill parish church in 1905 (Ulster Museum, Belfast)*

It was the landlord who directed the whole operation and provided the sole authority. Under his patent from the crown he was responsible for both civil government and criminal jurisdiction in his manor courts as well as the administration of Lurgan market and fairs. Even if his town had flourished there was little or no prospect of the townspeople ever acquiring responsibility for its government because the Dublin parliament had already created all the boroughs it required for political purposes and granted them corporate status: Lurgan was to develop as an estate town. Although the landlord alone was responsible for allocating and leasing properties to his tenants the terms of the plantation scheme prevented him from behaving towards them in an arbitrary manner. While Brownlow was permitted to retain 450 acres for his personal demesne, he was required to lease out the remainder: his leases had to run for a minimum of twenty-one years or a period of three lives named in the lease. Within the next twelve years four separate government commissions inspected all the estates and reported especially about the number of freeholders and leassees and the extent of lands they held. This applied not only in the countryside but also in the towns.

The 1622 survey recorded about Lurgan that there were then forty houses in a good village 'inhabited with English tenants, on both sides the streets, in which a good windmill stands'. It was also pointed out that even the 'cottagers' had 'some land to their houses for twenty-one years and some for longer terms'. In fact a paper submitted by Brownlow to the commissioners records 47 individual townsmen owning 57 houses and almost 1,500 acres. Of these acres about 1,000, or two-thirds of the total, were held by ten individuals, 340 by another twelve, and the remaining 144 by twenty-five: a social hierarchy had been born. The bulk of these lands lay in several townlands immediately adjacent to the town and were known as the townparks. These parcels of land were enclosed into small fields or parks with ditches and hawthorn hedges by the townspeople who leased them for tillage and pasture: there were no common lands for the use of the townspeople. Two townlands, defined as glebe for the parish church, would prevent development of the town towards the north-west for more than two centuries. Along each side of the main street and market place the land was divided up into tenements, plots of land fronting on the main street and running away down slopes to boundaries, formed on the western side by a stream and on the eastern side by an extent of bogland. Some of the larger tenements were several acres in extent and most, if not all, would have contained farmyards. Nothing is known about the buildings on these tenements – except a comment in a 1613 report about 'framed' houses – nor the conditions under which they were leased, because none of the pre-1641 leases have survived. An annotated transcript of the 1635 rent roll, however, in identifying several of the late seventeenth-century properties with those of the earlier period, reveals considerable continuity and suggests that many of the property boundaries were staked out in the early years of the town. They were

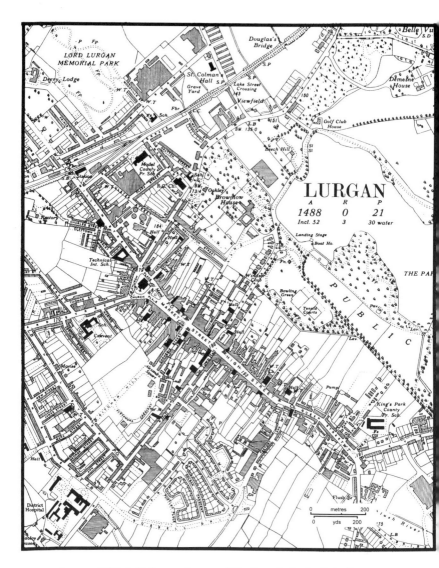

*Lurgan 1953-4, Ordnance Survey of Northern Ireland, six inches to one mile*

100

permanent features in its subsequent development.

The first stage of Lurgan's history ended with the 1641 rising. Lurgan was one of the first settlements to be attacked. After the loss of either sixteen or eighteen men (according to conflicting depositions) and a siege of a fortnight, Sir William Brownlow surrendered his castle and was imprisoned. Other depositions recount that the wall around the castle was razed and that the town was partially burned. Sir William survived the war and as early as 1648 he granted a new lease of a major property in the town. Although, however, he granted more leases in the 1650s (twenty-six of which survived into the late 1660s), it is significant that of sixty surnames listed in a 1635 rental, only six survived by 1659.

When Sir William Brownlow died in 1661 he was succeeded by his grandson Arthur Chamberlain, who was a minor. Arthur was required to assume the surname Brownlow and took over the estate in 1666. By the close of that year he had granted as many as 74 leases, 49 of them in the town. Just over half of the town leases were provisional leases for five to ten years but of twenty-two leases for lives or for twenty-one years, sixteen contained contracts for the tenants to build houses. The kind of house that Brownlow specified he sometimes described as an 'English house'. Its length ranged from twenty to thirty-six feet and its breadth from sixteen to twenty. As the foundation of the walls was required to be two or three feet high of stone and lime, the remaining structure must have been timber cage-work with plaster infill roughcasted with lime. The height was defined as either nine or ten feet with an oak loft and one or more chimneys of brick and stone. Within a few years, however, Brownlow was specifying stone gables and often also stone walls, while he was also insisting on a building line: it is clear that he was contemplating future infilling between the detached houses. In 1672, for example, William Mathews, a shopkeeper, agreed 'to build a house 29 feet in length ranging with Blackhall's and uniform thereto with a brick chimney and stone gavel [gable] covered with shingles, tiles or slates ...' When another shopkeeper, John Calvert, wanted to build a house on the frontstead next door they agreed to build over a gateway and Mathews was granted 'free liberty to lay joyces [joists] into the said John Calvert's gable end eight feet from the ground and from thence upward to the roof to join and build on the said gable end ...' Because the back-yards of many of these tenements were used for farming, trades, crafts or businesses, agreements had to be made to share these gateways. They became a feature of the Lurgan townscape and influenced subsequent building developments behind the frontsteads.

Another feature of Lurgan at this time was the shingled roof. Large wooden slates were considered superior to thatch and were especially common where wood was plentiful. In 1703 it was claimed that Lurgan was 'a large village consisting of a great many stone houses well shingled and finished ...' Twenty years earlier, a commentator on the barony of Oneilland, in which Lurgan lay, had asserted: 'the great plenty of oak wood ... makes our houses much better than those of other parts where that assistance is wanting.' This abundance of timber in the late seventeenth century is indicated throughout the English-settled districts of north Armagh and the Lagan valley by many references to shingled roofs. As late as 1777 the *Hibernian Magazine* noted that Lurgan contained '400 or 500 stone houses, the greatest number of which are covered with shingles or thatched, very few being slated'.

Lurgan became one of the more successful towns of Ulster in the late seventeenth century. It shared in the growing prosperity of the Lagan valley which developed a considerable dairying industry with increasing exports of butter, tallow and hides through Belfast. The rents of Lurgan's market tolls and customs doubled between 1658 and 1675 and trebled again by 1702. A substantial market house with cellars and two shops had been erected at one end of the market place by 1680. Contemporaries were more impressed, however, with the rise of a linen industry in Ulster. In 1682 Colonel Richard Lawrence, who had managed a linen manufactory at Chapelizod near Dublin for the duke of Ormond, gave it as his considered opinion that 'there is not a greater quantity of linen produced in like circuit of Europe [as in

Ulster]: and although the generality of their cloth fourteen years since was sleazy and thin, yet of late it is much improved to be a good fineness and strength.' About the same time a Portadown clergyman reckoned that in and about Lurgan was managed the greatest linen manufacture in Ireland. This phenomenon was related to heavy immigration from the north of England into the Lagan valley and north Armagh so that almost all the local surnames connected with the industry were English. Some of the early bleach yards were set up in the backsides of the Lurgan tenements. A significant encouragement to the trade must have been given by the landlord, Arthur Brownlow, who was able to claim later that 'on his first establishing the trade here, [he] bought up everything that was brought to the market of cloth and lost at first considerably; but at length, the thing fixing itself, he is now by the same methods a considerable gainer ...'

Probably of even more importance to Lurgan's immediate future was Brownlow's decision not to desert Lurgan during the Williamite wars: his attendance at the patriot parliament of 1689 and his subsequent liaison with the Williamite forces saved his town from serious damage. Although there was some dislocation among the tenants there is no evidence that property suffered. Indeed, in the immediate aftermath of the war the town continued to grow. The Friends' meeting house had to be rebuilt in 1695, and in 1697 a balcony was added to increase the accommodation in the parish church. The most spectacular development occurred around the market place. In 1696 Brownlow leased out ground next to the market house and within the next thirty years five more buildings were erected to form the Middle Row over a distance of some sixty yards towards the market green at the northern end. By 1725 a new parish church was erected on the green. Around the market place as well many of the older tenements were subdivided as leases expired and the houses along the front street were rebuilt to the highest standards specified by Brownlow when he took over the estate in 1666. In return he granted leases for terms of three lives and offered the tenants the opportunity to renew each lease at the fall of a life on payment of a year's rent as a renewal fine. These leases were in effect perpetuities. Yet whereas Arthur Brownlow had granted them very sparingly in the twenty-five years before 1690 – only twelve – he and his son William, who succeeded him, granted thirty-eight in the next thirty years. The largest number granted in any year was six in 1711, the year that Arthur died. These leases effectively freed their owners from landlord control because such tenants could not be evicted easily: even for non-payment of rents or fines they faced no worse than an action for debt. This policy enhanced the value of the property for sale or mortgage. In 1761, for example, one of the Middle Row properties was sold for £106 while in 1797 the very commodious Black Bull inn was sold to two Belfast merchants for £570. Indeed, throughout the eighteenth century, merchants could accumulate substantial holdings of such properties throughout the province as security for loans and debts.

Throughout the seventeenth century Lurgan developed as a Protestant town. A clause in leases insisted that leases could be 'alienated', or transferred by sale or mortgage, to British tradesmen only, giving the landlord first refusal. In religious allegiance the majority of the townspeople were members of the Church of Ireland and they attended the parish church of Shankill where Arthur Brownlow was very active. This church stood on the site of the pre-plantation church just north of the town and a balcony was added to it in 1697. In 1710 permission was obtained from parliament to erect a larger church on a new site and the market green was chosen: the building, which was consecrated in 1725, was rebuilt in 1863 and its tall spire still dominates the main street. Prominent in the early history of the town were the Quakers, for the first meeting of the Society of Friends in Ireland was founded in Lurgan in 1653. Although the number of Quakers was never large, the sect was very influential and contained many families prominent in the pioneering days of the domestic linen industry such as the Turners, Hoopes, Greers, Bradshaws and Christys. In the aftermath of the Williamite wars they decided 'to build a meeting house fit for a province meeting or other large meeting – the usual one formerly made use of being too little and going to decay...' In contrast with the strength of the Quakers was the weakness of a Presbyterian congregation in the town: as late as 1731 they had to supplicate the synod to continue its financial support for their poor congregation. A century later, however, they were able to build a substantial church. The first Methodist chapel in Lurgan was opened by John Wesley in 1778 and the growing congregation made it necessary to rebuild twice, first in 1802 and then again in 1826. Three years earlier in 1823 a Primitive Methodist church had been built and in 1856 they moved to a larger building. It was not until the year 1800 that the first Roman Catholic place of worship opened on the edge of the town when Charles Brownlow presented the local Roman Catholics with an old disused mill: it was reconditioned and served as a church until 1833.

Until the 1830s Lurgan's character did not change significantly because it reflected the town's reputation as the largest public market for fine linens in Ulster. In 1776 Arthur Young attended the market with Mr Brownlow:

> The cambrics are sold early, and through the whole morning; but when the clock strikes eleven the drapers jump upon stone standings, and the weavers flock about them with their pieces ... The draper's clerk stands by him, and writes his master's name on the pieces he buys, with the price; and, giving it back to the seller, he goes to the draper's quarters and waits his coming. At twelve it ends; then there is an hour for measuring the pieces, and paying the money; for nothing but ready money is taken; and this is the way the business is carried on at all the markets.

Ready money for the markets was provided by the agent of the Brownlow estate who used his rent receipts to purchase bills of exchange from the linen-drapers and even borrowed guineas from Dublin in the busiest seasons. The other needs of the travelling drapers for temporary offices and accommodation were provided by several inns that advertised their facilities in the *Belfast News Letter*: the Black Bull, the White Hart, the Hand and Hammer, the Cross Keys, the Spread Eagle, the Sign of the Bear, the Sign of the Cock, and the Brownlow's Arms. Although the built-up area of the town did not increase during this period, the density of population did and much building took place in the backsides of the tenements.

The major factor in the growth of Lurgan after 1830 was the invention of machinery to spin fine linen yarns. Although none of these new spinning mills was built in Lurgan, the volume of cheaper yarn that they produced gave a great boost to the handloom weavers of fine linens, especially those in the cambric trade for which Lurgan was famous. Even when the improvement of power-looms made it profitable to build several weaving factories in the town, Lurgan's major role in the linen industry continued to be the organisation of putting-out work throughout Ulster. In 1888 it was reckoned that Lurgan firms supplied almost 18,000 handloom weavers and several thousand more women engaged in white embroidery as far away as Donegal, while there were 2,500 employed in the power-loom factories and preparation departments for handloom weaving, and 2,500 employed in hem-stitching handkerchiefs by sewing machine. There were at least fifty firms in Lurgan engaged in the handkerchief trade including the hem-stitchers, finishers and printers.

As a result of the expansion of this branch of the linen industry the population of Lurgan rose from just over 2,800 in 1831 to 7,700 in 1861. Ten years later in 1871 it was 10,600 after a boundary change had increased the area from 120 to 850 acres. The population density of the surrounding countryside remained very high until well into the twentieth century. Lurgan was one of the first towns to take advantage of the 1828 act to elect town commissioners and later of the 1854 act that increased their powers. Both the landlord and the agent played a very active role in the improvement of the town and the provision of amenities such as water, sewerage, markets, cemeteries and fire-fighting. Lurgan secured both the union workhouse and the district model school. The town commissioners were responsible for promoting two major land developments. The new Ulster Railway reached Lurgan in 1841 and its station was built beside the crossing over the road to Lough Neagh. With the road to Antrim a suburb was thus demarcated that already contained the new

Catholic parish church of St Peter (1833). By the late 1840s it also had the model school, the courthouse, and the new gas works. On the other side of the market place another suburb developed on the Church of Ireland glebe lands, some twenty years before the disestablishment of the Church of Ireland.

One of the most surprising features of this expansion was the rapid growth of Catholic church properties in these districts under the direction of a succession of vigorous clerics. Dr O'Brien, who had been responsible in the 1830s for the building of St Peter's church, lived to see the addition of a chancel and transepts in 1869. He was responsible too for bringing the Sisters of Mercy from Newry in the mid-1860s to take charge of education and several schools were built as well as a convent overlooking the market place. As a result the east-west axis formed by the roads to Portadown and Antrim assumed a Catholic character.

Lurgan town continued to grow slowly but steadily until the beginning of the second world war. Its specialised linen industry suffered severely from competition first from cotton and later from the introduction of paper handkerchiefs and napkins. Yet the handloom damask industry survived into the 1960s, producing superb table linens fit for royalty. Lurgan still weaves fine linens and is famous for its textile printing. But it required a wider manufacturing base. The Craigavon project was designed to provide this as well as an attractive environment.

**Select bibliography**
R. G. Gillespie: *Settlement and Survival on an Ulster Estate: the Brownlow Leasebook 1667–1711*, Belfast, 1988
F. X. McCorry: *Lurgan: An Irish Provincial Town 1610-1970*, Lurgan, 1993

*Ennistymon and the River Cullenagh (Local Studies Centre)*

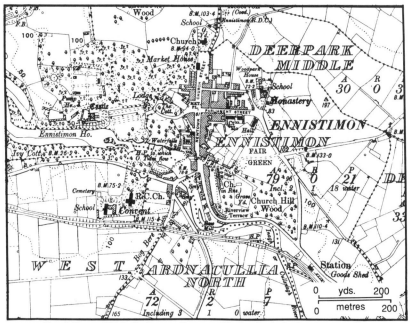

*Ennistimon 1916, Ordnance Survey of Ireland, six inches to one mile.*
*[The Ordnance Survey spelling 'Ennistimon' has not been generally*
*accepted]*

# ENNISTYMON

*Margaret MacCurtain*

ENNISTYMON sits on a saucer-shaped depression in the southern threshold of the region of Clare which contains the Burren. The main approaches to this medium-sized market town afford different perspectives of its structure. Travelling from Ennis the main road winds between drumlin hills following the route of the River Cullenagh with occasional glimpses of the settlement clustered in a hollow below eye level. Ennistymon's most celebrated physical feature is its river bend of gently-falling water cascading over the wide limestone slabs of the river, the Falls of Ennistymon. A compact grey-stone town, its response to its riverline setting lends a charming intimacy to its unfolding brightly-painted streetscapes as the eye follows the upland slopes at the edges of the town.

From the Lahinch road the town comes into view arranging itself around the bridge which forms its core and then purposefully it occupies the river bank east of the crossing, its buildings backing the river. On the opposite side, cut off from the Lahinch road by the river, stands the Falls Hotel incorporating Ennistymon House, the former landlord's Georgian mansion which was built on the ruins of an O'Brien castle. Positioned on a rocky knoll and set against a woodland backdrop, the present hotel was home to the MacNamaras whose 18,000-acre estate included the town in the last century. Looking down on Ennistymon from the hills on the northern extremity of the town, its schematic layout demonstrates how well the designers of the town adapted roof lines and street junctions to the spatial limitations of a scooped-out hollow. Built by the best stone-masons of Ireland, there is a congruence of shape and form about this place which comes from a long tradition of knowing how to express vernacular art in stone.

Ennistymon's name has been variously rendered as

'Diamain's river meadow' and as 'the island of the middle house', each name recalling disputed folkloric theories concerning its origins. In the medieval period a shadowy St Luchtighern was reputed to have a monastic settlement in the parish close to the shallow ford of the river near the Falls. Looking across the river at the present-day Falls Hotel from the summit of Church Hill the viewer has no difficulty in recognising an earlier settlement pattern of castle, mill, river ford and dwelling-houses. The references to the moated O'Connor castle at 'Inisdyman' date back to an entry for 1422 in the *Annals of the Four Masters*. We may conjecture that this important settlement was well fortified. North-west Clare in the late middle ages was studded with tower-houses and fortified castles. In the late Elizabethan period Ennistymon castle passed into the possession of the O'Briens, the local aristocratic family who held it for over two centuries. In the *Books of Survey and Distribution for County Clare* compiled for the Cromwellian settlement after the confederate wars in the mid-seventeenth century, the townland of Ennistymon and its castle then belonging to the O'Briens are itemised. A survey of 1703 by Thomas Moland notes that 'the farm of Inishtimond ... is a manor and has on it a good castle and a house joining to it two storeys high and in good repair, a stable and other convenient outhouses, with a small garden, a corn mill and seven or eight cabins.' Sometime later the castle was renovated in a Georgian style and in the following century its occupants at that period, the Finucanes, added the west wing. When the Rev. James Kenny, archdeacon of Kilfenora, arrived in the 1770s to open up the area to the Church of Ireland he found three miserable cabins attached to the mansion of Edward O'Brien on the far side of the river.

The construction of the fine stone bridge with its seven arches, which is still in use, took place during the closing decades of the eighteenth century. This was the crucial factor in the growth of the town: to this day its original core extends from Bridge Street to the old market house and from there the main axis slopes up Church Street to the handsome Protestant church, St Andrew's.

Gradually as Ennistymon advanced into the nineteenth century the town expanded its business and commercial interests in response to the demands of the agricultural economy of its hinterland. A lively export trade in horses and heifers continued even after the end of the Napoleonic wars in 1815. By then cattle were being brought from the midlands to be fattened on the grasslands of east Clare on the edge of the Burren. Fairs began to take place at regular intervals throughout the year and Ennistymon became the centre for markets in eggs, potatoes, oats and after the mid-century large quantities of butter. Shops and public houses were built with the craftsmanship associated traditionally with the stone masonry of the region. The art of drystone walling which is a feature of many of the buildings and walls of the town bears testimony to the local pride of the mason-architect of County Clare. Ennistymon at no time allowed itself to surrender its independent air of self-suf-ficiency to the rental book of the landlord and to the unifor-mity of estate cottages. During and after the Napoleonic wars the town took off as one of the chief market towns of Munster and in the second half of the nineteenth century it operated two weekly markets, mainly of butter, as well as hosting six large cattle and pig fairs throughout the year.

By 1824 Ennistymon had a population of 1,500 and the street-names reflect the town's expansion. The toll-house on the bridge admitted the traveller from the Liscannor coast to Oldtown Street whence the traffic moved without a break into Newtown Street and Market Place. From the late eight-eenth century Ennistymon possessed a jail and session house. To this day the session house stands at the junction of Market Place and Parliament Street, which also housed the courthouse and constitutional hall. Church Hill and Bog-berry Street were amongst the earliest streets housing the employees of the landlord's estate, tradesmen and workers.

Religion played a role in the development of Ennisty-mon and the position and setting of its main ecclesiastical buildings tell their own story. In 1776 the Rev. James Kenny used the small church and cemetery on the crest of Church Street, now a neglected but still significant focus on the rim of the saucer which contains the town's centre. By the 1790s the town had 120 houses, seventy of which were slated. It is not certain when the Anglican church was moved to a north-west position overlooking the town along Church Street. Samuel Lewis, the nineteenth-century topographer, gives its date as 1830: 'a handsome cruciform structure, in the later English style, with an octagonal tower on its south side resting on a square base' is how he described St Andrew's church. It has recently been acquired as a Teach Ceoil, a music centre for the region, by Comhaltas Ceoltoirí.

Although the Rev. Kenny declared that he saw no evidence of a church presence for Roman Catholics when he arrived at the hamlet, an unusual amalgamation of two medieval parishes, Kilmanaheen and Clouna, was even then taking place, putting pressure on the Catholic church authorities to make provision for the sizeable worshipping population by providing a chapel for their needs. The nascent town happened to be situated where the two parishes met to form the new parish of Ennistymon and the first chapel occupies a location high over Main Street which was made over to the Christian Brothers when they took up residence in 1824. This then became Mount St Joseph, consisting of the Brothers' monastery, a primary school, and later a secondary school of distinction, a landscaped compound pleasing to the eye.

With the expansion of the town the Catholic church was moved to a commanding site on the Lahinch road looking out over the town across to the landlord's mansion. Built on a terrace, this was later extended by the addition of the classically proportioned convent and schools which the Sisters of Mercy had designed for them by M. A. Hennessy, the architect, in 1874. Spatially the ecclesiastical buildings of Ennistymon play a significant part in defining the zones and limits of the town. The Mercy sisters conducted a school for the girls of Ennistymon in Bridge House, which became the residence of the Griffin family. One of the rooms used to be the oratory and has a stained-glass window. The *Clare Journal* of 1 August 1872 refers to Colonel MacNamara giving them a valuable site for a new convent school at the end of Parliament Street but in fact the convent was built on the hill and by 1878 it was given its status as Ennistymon convent.

Despite the prosperity of Ennistymon at the beginning of the nineteenth century there was a grave crisis in the economy of County Clare and along the western seaboard due in large measure to the rising population. Potato shortages seemed chronic and fever epidemics a recurring feature of those early decades of the nineteenth century, culminating in the great famine. The census of 1841 shows the population of County Clare as over a quarter of a million with 26,650 families living in one-roomed cabins constructed of mud. The potato was diet and livelihood to the cottier. Several years previous to the ominous statistic, a commission of enquiry into the state of the poor in Ireland had warned the government that in the event of the failure of the potato crop in any particular year a famine would prevail. In 1838 the government scheme known as the workhouses system was set up with a wide brief to relieve the destitute throughout the country. County Clare was divided into four poor law unions of which Ennistymon union, created in August 1839, had responsibility for the baronies of Corcomroe and Burren. Its 238 square miles had a population of 46,637. For levying purposes the electoral divisions of Ennistymon union were spread over nine parishes.

As in many other areas around the country a workhouse was built in Ennistymon. It was opened in 1842 and occupied a magnificent location overlooking Liscannor Bay. Built of cut stone on the specifications of government plans, the main building was two storeys high with matching outbuildings that housed chapel, fever hospital and general infirmary. The striking classical design of the workhouse concealing its inner severity came to dominate the Liscannor entrance to Ennistymon for upwards of eighty years. Through its great central reception door, which separated the female section on the right from the male section on the left with the children removed to the upper parts, were to file thousands of frightened, starved and fevered victims of famine and destitution.

The Ennistymon workhouse was built to accommodate 870 inmates. However in 1847 the average number of inmates per month was 600 and the number of deaths 961. By October 1848, 2,200 were passing through its entrance door monthly and auxiliary workhouses had to be opened in outlying districts. By February 1850 there were over 2,500 people in the various workhouses of the Ennistymon union. Between 1847 and 1851, 4,996 people had died, many of cholera, according to the handwritten record books. Though few traces of the workhouse now remain, there is a small stonewalled cemetery, no longer in use, set in a sloping field called the children's graveyard, a sad memorial to that grim period. The workhouse was demolished in the 1920s and replaced by a cheerful cottage hospital. For the townspeople of Ennistymon the workhouse was a place of dread and tragedy, yet paradoxically a source of employment and commerce. Maggie Davis, at present the oldest inhabitant in the town, now in her hundredth year, recalls the memories of her childhood. 'Oh Lord, oh Lord, the washing the women from the town used have to do, it was terrible. They had to wash them anyhow. The sheets'd be all hanging out on the line branded "Ennistymon Workhouse".'

Griffith's valuation of 1855 supplies many clues about the economic life of the town as it recovered from the famine. There were approximately 241 houses dispersed throughout seven streets and the several lanes and roads leading off those streets. The number of businesses was listed as twenty-seven, eight clustering in Church Street and six in Newtown Street. An emerging middle class comprising shopkeepers and business people had shifted the centre of social activity away from the older areas of Church Hill and Bogberry. The construction of the Buttermarket shortly after the mid-century marked a new stage in the development of the town. Its main street frontage was allocated an open space and commanded a vista looking southward. A building of some character, its air of bustling commerce and its huge firkin-making industry gave Ennistymon butter market the reputation for many decades of being second in importance only to Cork. By the 1880s the town was prosperous. *Guy's Postal Directory of Munster* for 1886 informs the reader that the business enterprises of Ennistymon comprised vintners, grocers, victuallers, drapers, bakers, flour and meal dealers, egg merchants, hardware merchants, leather dealers, oil and colour merchants as well as tailors and outfitters. Numerically this list can be broken down to 24 vintners, 37 grocers, 8 bakers, 5 victuallers, 7 hardware merchants, 5 seed merchants, 19 flour and meal dealers and 6 car-owners.

Businesses tended to be family-owned, several remaining in the same family for more than one generation. The town had its own woollen mills and supplied the whole country with knitted socks, as well as friezes, tweeds and flannels. The trades too were well represented. There were eight bootmakers, three carpenters, five coopers, two saddlers, four blacksmiths renowned in north-west Clare for the style and quality of their gates, and a coachbuilder of considerable reputation. A number of dressmakers, and six tailors were supplemented by a large domestic industry in crochet, lace and knitwork. There was one hotel, Daly's commercial and family hotel, situated in Parliament Street. Fair days were big social events with public houses overflowing and cattle standing everywhere around the market place. An air of jocularity pervaded the atmosphere and the fair green just north of the town was full of wonderful baubles from the ends of the earth to satisfy child and adult.

The shop-fronts of Ennistymon are quite spectacular and are justly regarded as among the best surviving specimens of Irish vernacular street art. Each front had its own distinctive colours, painted on pitch-pine beams washed up on Clare beaches from some long-forgotten wreckage, or so the legend goes. The grain of wood and the artistry of the design combine with a rich variety of colours to give the street facades acclaimed recognition by photographers and artists. The printing of names overhead and the wooden setting of lintels and shutters are details that delight the observer. They are prized for the antique value they possess, possibly deriving from a time when a shop required a memorable colour scheme to lure a customer back again, and they are carefully restored when in need of repair.

In the census of 1891 the population of Ennistymon was 1,200. In that year the new post office opened, taking money orders and parcels as well as operating a telegraph office. The building of the West Clare railway in the 1880s gave Ennistymon an advantage over other towns in the Burren region, though Lisdoonvarna's Improvements Committee, promoting the popular spa there, had the temerity to describe Ennistymon as 'the station on the West Clare line where you get out for Lisdoonvarna'. For the townspeople the station with its two platforms was a fresh lease of life. Cattle could be hoisted up and transported in all directions. Later milk churns went up and down the line. Butter was loaded on horse-drawn floats at the market house and brought to the extensive goods yard adjoining the pretty station on the Ennis road. The returning floats delivered merchandise and orders to the shops. The railway station was always bustling. There were four trains each way daily, one being the mail train. Percy French immortalised the West Clare railway, catching the element of hazard as it made its way precariously across the boggy moorland, reaching its summit level of 250 feet and then falling gradually towards Ennistymon. 'Your're in luck if you reach Ennistymon, for all the way home is downhill'. An older inhabitant recalls the wheels creating their own rhythm: 'diddly-dum, diddly-dum, diddly-dum, diddly dum', then as it began to climb, 'diddeely dum-um, dum', followed by a perceptible and ominous pause, after which it renewed its 'diddlydum, diddly-dum', quickening as it came in sight of the town. Passengers from Milltown Malbay, Quilty and Corofin came to shop in Ennistymon. During the summer holidays swarms of children paid threepence to go to Lahinch for a swim. Ennistymon's empire stretched from the Aran Islands to Quilty in that blissful far-off time before the coming of the motor car. The railway line was finally closed in 1962. There are many who would wish to see it opened up again.

The Falls Hotel occupies a special position via-a-vis the town, enviable in a number of respects. Possibly the knowledge that the last of the MacNamaras, Francis, came back to his ancestral home in 1936 and opened the family property as a hotel gave back to the town its invisible matrix. For a brief period the hotel was a literary haven associated with the poet Dylan Thomas and the artist Augustus John through marriages with the daughters of Francis Mac-Namara. After the second world war, J. F. Wood, the new owner, constructed a hydro-electric plant on the Falls which supplied the hotel with its own electricity. The MacNamaras had inherited the estate from the Finucanes and throughout the nineteenth century their relationship with the town was unobtrusively generous. When land was needed for development they gave it, and their best monument to the town was the construction of Victoria Terrace set high on Church Hill, consisting of a landscaped terrace of well-built cottages fitting snugly into the general topography of the area.

Irish was the spoken language in this part of Clare until the third quarter of the nineteenth century when, with the pressure of emigration and modernisation, spoken English asserted itself. Brian Merriman, the author of *The Midnight Court*, was almost certainly born in Ennistymon where his father, a stone-mason, was employed. Whole sections of Merriman's great poem were recited from memory on festive occasions. Traditional music and storytelling formed a strong chain of entertainment between families in Ennistymon: the Madigans, the Arthurs, the O'Dwyers and the Ahernes were much in demand all over the country. Up in Church Hill the Byrts, the Walshs and the McCormacks held a musical tradition over decades. The Corcomroe and Burren baronies possessed bardic schools of poetry in the middle ages and the scribal arts of manuscript writing and recording as well as Irish poetry were taught for over five centuries. Between 1700 and 1850 the work of an estimated fifty poets writing in Irish in County Clare has been located, at least five of whom were inhabitants of Ennistymon. Public recitation of poetry was a feature of the town's social life and is by no means defunct. Instinctively nationalist in sympathy, the publicans of Ennistymon were the first to raise the tricolour over their doors in 1917 as the townspeople gave their assent to the bid for independence in the following years. Shops and houses were burnt down by crown forces but with the resumption of peace the town again entered a period of prosperity. The installation of electricity came early in the 1930s, hastened by the government's decision to give an important creamery to the town. With it came public lighting, running water and a new sewage system.

In 1829, the year of Catholic emancipation, Ennistymon parish held 19,000 people; in the 1986 census it had 3,000. Over the last thirty years the town has been drained of many of its young people. Improved educational opportunities combined with an inability to provide employment have removed a vital middle layer of the town's population. Since the early 1960s the chamber of commerce has worked hard on its policy of attracting industry to the town. Two factories failed, but one electronic company employing young people is a successful local venture. In general the incentive to develop full-time employment does not match the perception that to be a recipient of state unemployment assistance is attractive in a region where tourism offers opportunities for seasonal casual labour.

Yet Ennistymon remains at the centre of the region's commercial life. The weekly Tuesday market has expanded to meet the needs of tourists: boxes of exotic fruit compete with home-grown vegetables and house plants. Rows of bright cottons range beside the small currency of technology, electronic watches and batteries. Two fish passes have been created on the river close to the Falls to enable salmon to go upstream, thus opening up twenty-seven miles of river and lake fishing.

Business is still family-owned. Fitzpatrick's supermarket in Parliament Street brings the out-of-town shopper who stays to eat. A thriving bakery and tea shop, the creation of a Bavarian baker and his Clare wife, is always full. Two local women run a brisk trade in knitwear carrying on the local designs and employing outdoor knitters as in former times. High quality leatherwork has always been a valued craft here, indeed Wall's shoe and boot factory, now closed, trained great shoemakers for decades. How to tap the immense creativity of this region is the key to its future employment structure.

Ennistymon is a town in harmony with its environment. Its newer housing estates fit into the hilly slopes, and ribbon development is restrained along the main access roads. There is a sense of growing communal awareness. A centre for young people runs Fás programmes which are realistic. There is a day care centre for the elderly. The fire station is a recent installation and the garda station, one of the four district headquarters of County Clare with its own superintendent, was relocated to a larger building on the Ennis side of the town some years ago. A busy public library reflects the concern of the 1980s with heritage and culture. Ennistymon is a town to return to if you were fortunate enough to be born there, and if you are endowed with brains in your hands, to live in Ennistymon is to relish the language of building materials and the pattern of stone walls.

**Select bibliography**
*British Parliamentary Papers, Famine Ireland*, vols. 3, 5, Irish University Press, Dublin, 1969
W. Nolan: *North West Clare today? Tomorrow?* Report commissioned by North West Clare Development Organisation, Ennis, 1979
*A Guide to Ennistymon Union 1839–1850*, A North Clare Historical Society/Fás community response project. Project supervisor M. Comber, North Clare Historical Society, 1992
P. Ó Laoi: 'The parish of Ennistymon', *Ennistymon Parish Magazine*, 1986, pp. 3-6
D. Fitzpatrick: *Politics and Irish Life, 1913–21*, Dublin, 1977

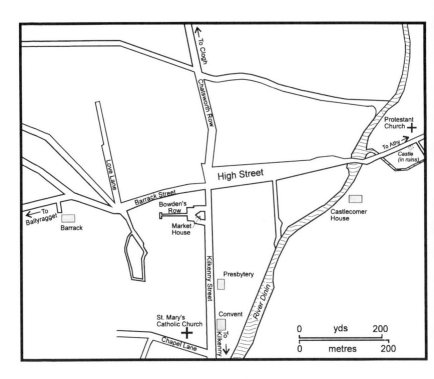

*Castlecomer, based on Ordnance Survey of Ireland, six inches to one mile, 1902*

# CASTLECOMER

### William Nolan

CASTLECOMER in north County Kilkenny is a junction where shale meets limestone, hill meets lowland and miner meets farmer. Two family streams flow through the history of the town and its hinterland – the O'Brennans of Idough and the Wandesfordes of Kirklington in Yorkshire. The early history of settlement here is shadowy and obscure. Some claim that the O'Brennans had a rath close to the *cumar* (gorge) where the Brockagh, Cloghogue and Dinin rivers meet and it was transformed to a motte on which William Marshall, one of the great Anglo-Norman magnates, placed a wooden castle, the castle of the *cumar* or water gorge – hence Castlecomer as the name of the place. Traces of early settlement have been obliterated by subsequent rebuilding and demesne development but the proximity of pre-medieval parish church and motte suggests that here was the centre of the manor granted to the de Valle family in the early twelfth century. Apart from Castlecomer, which the Anglo-Norman documents invariably refer to as a *castrum*, and Ballyragget west on the Nore, there was no substantial urban development in north Kilkenny. Castlecomer was never more than a military outpost in the medieval period and has none of the texture of places such as Thomastown, Callan, Gowran or Inistioge.

Records from 1359 and 1400 suggest that the O'Brennans were regarded as an independent force who made agreements with the Butlers on equal terms. Subsequent history demonstrates the gradual absorption of their territory by the earl of Ormond and his Kilkenny-city satellite merchant families of Rothe, Archer and Shee.

From the late sixteenth to the mid-seventeenth century a cadre of itinerant civil servants, tax-collectors and speculators descended on the O'Brennan lands. 'This part of Kilkenny', wrote a surveyor in 1584, 'doth border with Upper

Ossory and Leix and in another part thereof with the Kavanaghs and was by occasion of divers spoils and preys subject to waste and also remote from the sea'. Defects of geography linked to political instability made it a prime target for speculators. In 1614 the O'Brennans surrendered their lands to Black Tom, tenth earl of Ormond, champion of the reformation, monarchy and common law. Regranted under surrender and entrapped by a new legal system they were especially vulnerable to a group of powerful politicians who were unceasing in their search for lucrative investments in the early seventeenth century. Between 1600 and 1636 the O'Brennan lands passed through three grantees before being finally sold to Sir Christopher Wandesforde, master of the rolls in the administration of Thomas Strafford, earl of Wentworth, on 5 July 1636. Before that the lawyers had decreed by inquisition that the O'Brennans, as mere Irish, were intruders who had held their homeland by force of arms notwithstanding the fact that it had passed to the king on the demise of Strongbow's posterity. Why was there such an interest in this remote place? The answer lies in the perception that iron ore and woodland would fuel in north Kilkenny the kind of industrial revolution which was making men prosperous in contemporary Britain. All the participants in the race for Idough had interests in the infant iron industry in Ireland, and the political influence to win monopolies and concessions from central government.

In the turbulent politics of the period Christopher Wandesforde had little time to profit from his speculation. After the recall of Strafford in 1641, Wandesforde became lord deputy of Ireland but died in December of that year. If the years 1636–41 mark the foundation of the town of Castlecomer there is little extant evidence to indicate it. Claims made in 1653 by William Wandesforde to the commonwealth for the return to him of his brother's estate referred to 'coalpits, woods, iron works which were lying waste and inhabited by strangers and Irish not paying any rent'. Another witness specified that the late lord deputy had laid out £14,000 in the building of a market town with 'houses of lime and stone and other houses, several iron-works, impounding a great deer park'. The contemporaneous Down Survey map shows a bawn and castle and the Civil Survey only records a 'little stone house with iron mine and coal at Castlecomer'. The 1653 petition also asserted that five hundred English Protestants had been settled in Idough but that these had fled and the natives were now encouraging the return of priests to say mass. The 1659 'census' suggests that these claims were greatly exaggerated – Castlecomer had an adult population of 40 (4 English and 36 Irish) whereas Ballyragget, the only other major settlement in the barony, had 127 adults of whom 23 were English.

The exploitation of the iron and coal of Castlecomer's hinterland proceeded in the seventeenth century but there is little evidence of how mining impacted on the new central place. Gerard Boate in 1645 claimed that coal was discovered in the search for iron and other sources describe how in 1689 coal was hauled overland to the Barrow for transhipment to St Mullins and New Ross for the Dublin market. Samuel Molyneux in 1707, described the multitude of exhausted coal pits operated by specialist groups of colliers.

The town must have been a rudimentary urban place but the only evidence we have of landlord residence are the claims by tenants for monies due for the delivery of cheese, meat and wine to the occupants of the 'castle' at Castlecomer in 1739. A report on the estate in 1746 described Castlecomer as 'a very poor place for want of some manufacture or public business being carried on there which would increase the town and bring inhabitants to live there especially as there is a very good foot barracks and a river running through the town'. William Batwell's survey is concerned primarily with rural land but it does refer to rural middlemen and colliery officials investing in urban property. Batwell was forced to stay in the house of Richard Wright at Castlecomer because of the poor state of the inn and this Wright was middle tenant of two rural townlands.

A 1759 map depicts the demesne with plantations and the inevitable gazebo and a 1783 painting shows Castlecomer House to the east of the Dinin River. Castlecomer town belongs firmly to the late eighteenth century along with other north Kilkenny towns such as Freshford and Johnstown. Its formal layout with a central square, four intersecting streets, market house, big house, demesne and Church of Ireland church, Catholic chapel and cabin suburbs dates from the accession of Anne Wandesforde to the estate in 1784. She married John Butler of Garryricken thereby becoming countess of Ormond and inaugurating the most momentous phase of development in Castlecomer's history. The events of 1798 brought a sudden halt to building. On Friday 22 June in that year, Fr John Murphy of Boolavogue and Miles Byrne led their force of Wexfordmen and Doonane colliers in an attack on Comer. After an inconclusive battle the Wexfordmen departed leaving over a hundred casualties which included the clerk of the chapel. The main street of the town was in ruins and the Protestant church and big house were likewise destroyed. Some seventy townspeople put in claims for damages to housing and property. Lady Ormond claimed £8,000 for the destruction of Castlecomer House, plate, wines, library and paintings. Two other claimants, Robert Kane and William Wilkinson, had claims in excess of £1,000. Thirty townspeople alleged loss of houses and the evidence suggests that the major destruction was in Bridge Street and the Square – the core of the town.

Lady Ormond's compensation together with colliery profits, which in 1798 were estimated at £10,000, helped to reconstruct the town on a grand scale. Castlecomer House and St Mary's church were rebuilt and a market house fronted with Carlow limestone and a Palladian facade, a fever hospital, dispensary and houses for miners in Bowden's Row augmented the town's buildings. James Healy's map of 1812 shows a triangular-shaped town occupying the narrow area west of the Dinin and between the parallel north-south ridges of high ground. The town limits were sharply defined by either public buildings or physical landmarks.

Beyond the river, on low ground symbolically to the east, the big house of the Wandesfordes, estate farmyard and the Protestant church lay detached from the town proper. Westwards the infantry barracks on high ground guarded the approaches from the hills of Ballymartin and Byrnes-grove. The Catholic chapel was at the southern extremity just inside the town gates on the Kilkenny road and furthest distant of all town buildings from the big house. The Wandesforde manuscripts indicate that some seventy-two houses were built between 1796 and 1838. Only nine of these can be attributed directly to the countess of Ormond – six weavers' houses in Bowden's Row and three more substantial ones in Bridge Street. Fortunately it is possible to identify the people responsible for the building of Castlecomer town. In Bridge Street some twenty substantial houses, mainly on the northern side, were built by either prosperous rural middlemen, colliery personnel or managerial estate staff. The agent, Richard Eaton, lived here as did cartographer, canal engineer and mining expert David Aher. Here we find the houses of Joseph Bradley, colliery proprietor, Richard Reeche, the estate gardener, and Dr Hanford. Robert Kane, who survived summary trial by the Wexfordmen in 1798 and received over £1,000 in compensation, rebuilt his imposing house in a prime site on the square for a reputed cost of £3,000. Kane was the landlord of a cabin quarter in Chatsworth Street and derived his principal income through subletting 800 acres of rural land. Kilkenny Street adjoining the square had some substantial properties, mainly shops and pubs, but deteriorated southwards where another rural middleman, John Hendricken, had let sites for a 'great number of cabins comprising one side of the town's suburb' close to the Catholic chapel. The landlord's role was that of planning authority rather than town developer and the existence of long leases gave middlemen tenants discretionary rights over their sites. Castlecomer, therefore, is more properly defined as a middleman town.

After the death of the countess of Ormond her son John Wandesforde began a programme of rationalisation which was particularly successful in breaking the hold of middle interests in the town, collieries and rural land. By 1850 over half of the town's 262 housing units were in landlord hands. The landlord was also determined to prohibit any unsightly developments in the proximity of the big house and the demesne was particularly sacrosanct, thereby confining

Castlecomer's physical growth west of the Dinin and regulating the river to a peripheral role in the townscape. Estate regulations prohibited any interference with trees or grassland within a mile of the town and in 1843 the landlord expended a considerable sum in breaking Bartholomew Brophy's lease to lands along the river banks, which were commonly used for recreational purposes on Sundays or as the landlord claimed 'for desecrating the Sabbath'.

Landlord autonomy however was beginning to weaken. John O'Connell, son of the Liberator, represented Kilkenny city in parliament and nationalists and repealers controlled the corporation in 1843. In 1845 the repealers of Castlecomer defied the landlord, who had imposed sanctions on estate employees and tenants for attending O'Connell's mass meeting in Kilkenny, by building a 'commercial establishment' for John Bradley. The Catholic church became a major shaper of urban space. Paradoxically the spate of church building unleashed by emancipation continued unabated during the famine years. Castlecomer's Church of the Immaculate Conception, with its impressive east facade climaxing in twin spires, taken down in 1960, was built between 1844 and 1852. The church with its impressive bulk dominated the streetscape of a treeless Kilkenny Street. Local craftsmen such as the Hetherington family of plasterers were to embellish imported statuary and set the standards by which the work of future generations would be judged, at Sunday mass. Across the street the Presentation nuns had begun in 1829 to build up their educational enterprise. Theological animosity, diluted by the maternal rule of the countess of Ormond after 1798, became noticeably sharper during the famine years as landlord and parish priest hurled paper missives across the river. Conflict arose primarily over the landlord policy of assisted emigration which removed over 5,000 people from the estate and contributed to a reduction in estate population from 12,466 in 1841 to 6,317 in 1851. Wandesforde claimed that the estate would be bankrupted by uncontrolled growth whereas the Catholic clergy accused him of extirpating his Catholic tenantry. The *Kilkenny Journal* wrote that 'Hon. Mr Wandesforde shipped off 1,855 people from his estate in the year of our Lord 1847. He has ambitions of exercising almost unlimited despotism over his tenantry and has a strong propensity to thin the population and level the cabins of the poor as he levelled the ground and three-quarters of the town, which had grown up under Lady Ormond.'

The town's population however declined only from 1,765 to 1,724 but rural townlands adjoining which were the cabin suburbs showed a more drastic decline. Donaguile townland, for example, fell from 857 to 204 and the number of houses from 146 to 37. Somewhat belatedly in 1852 the last of Ireland's 163 workhouses built to contain hunger was opened in Donaguile close to the Catholic church. The board of guardians appointed John Wandesforde as chairman and Brennan of Eden Hall, claimant of the right to be called O'Brennan of Idough, as vice-chairman. The administration of poverty had sharpened the committee skills of the Catholic middle class and reduced their deference to landlords and agents. Henceforth, as Tom Lyng, the historian of Castlecomer, puts it succinctly, 'the parochial house was pushing against the big house and the boardroom of the workhouse was become a kind of local parliament'. With the trauma of famine past there were few changes to the Castlecomer townscape in the second half of the nineteenth century. Gradually the role of the landlord was being eroded by the assumption of health, welfare and housing responsibilities by the State.

The 1911 census returned a population of 1,129 for Castlecomer and Donaguile. The manuscript records reveal the more intimate social geography of the town and disprove the popular assumption that Castlecomer was both a mining and a Protestant town. Census figures show that the proportion of non-Catholics in Castlecomer parish was some eleven per cent, which is substantially greater than the four per cent recorded for County Kilkenny. An analysis of the figures for Castlecomer town shows that the non-Catholic population constituted nine per cent of the population. Obvious concentrations in the area of High Street and Chatsworth Row constituted the old core of the eighteenth-century town. The return also emphasises the essentially rural base of mining in the town – only 4 out of 189 heads of households were listed as miners.

Richard Henry Prior Wandesforde and his wife were away on the night of the census and their three children were in the care of ten servants including a housekeeper, nurse, cook, three housemaids, a scullery maid and a footman, none of whom were born locally. Across the road in the estate farm buildings two foresters, two gamekeepers, two coachmen and a gardener testified to landlord interest in trees, game, horses and roses. Across the bridge was the wide tree-lined street of relative privilege and respectability. High Street had the largest number of domestic servants, stables, coach houses, professional men and Protestants. One could encounter here Alfred Nicholas (bank official), Charlotte Cooper Chadwick (a lady on annuity), Sarah Martindale (teacher), T. W. Harpur (a clerk in holy orders) and Michael Harlow (a medical officer). Chatsworth Row was a more mixed street. One of its residents was Denis Carroll, clerk of the union, district councillor and employer of two servants. Close to him lived John Gleeson, a labourer, and John Brennan, a coachbuilder. Kilkenny Street was the centre of business, replete with shop assistants, skilled workers, labourers and nuns. John Beggin, grocer and baker with two shop assistants and two servants, rubbed shoulders with Catherine Treacy, described as a widow labouring outside, William Rainsford, a coal carrier, and Richard Meehan, clerk of the Catholic church, and fifteen nuns lived in the convent.

Lake Lane had a preponderance of labourers such as Michael Connell, coal miner, Michael Corcoran, and coal carters Tom Nolan and William McGrath. Bowden's Row was an enclave of craft workers with shoemakers Michael Maher and John Doyle, tinsmith Patrick Connell and harness-maker William O'Toole. Barrack Street on the hill had the only substantial lodging-houses in the town, run by Annie Armour, although John Dormer (peddler) managed to keep twelve lodgers in his premises. Few were unemployed in 1911. Family trades were common in wickerwork, carpentry, plastering and coach building.

The bulk of the estate lands of 20,000 acres were sold to

occupiers under the provisions of the 1903 land act and the Wandesfordes were thrown back on the coal which had lured them to Comer in 1636 and the town which it partly financed. Richard Henry Prior Wandesforde inherited the truncated estate in 1904 and became a passionate campaigner for the town. An inventive and energetic man, he assiduously promoted the town and Castlecomer coal and in 1918 secured the railway connection which the industry so badly needed. 'The Captain', as he was called locally, introduced commercial basket-making, the manufacture of perambulators, an agricultural bank, a colliery co-operative society and the local creamery in 1913. He became a district councillor and added Florence Terrace to the townscape of Kilkenny Street. Many Castlecomer people, urged on by the big house and played in by the local band, set off to fight in the first world war. A plaque in St Mary's church recalls those who never returned including the landlord's son. After 1916, loyalty to the big house and its politics wilted under pressure from Sinn Féin. The bands which drummed young men to France in 1914 now played at a massive anti-conscription rally in Castlecomer in 1918. In 1921 Captain Wandesforde withdrew from local politics and resigned from the local council over its policy of sending official returns to the Dáil Éireann rather than to the Custom House in Dublin.

In 1924 Deerpark colliery, sunk through the heart of the ornamental landscape so much guarded by his predecessors, symbolised Wandesforde's pragmatic approach. Generations of Castlecomer miners, now urbanised in new housing at Maryville beside the Catholic church, earned a hard living there but remember with affection the companionship of the pithead. The new century heralded the developing strength of workers, ably marshalled by Nixie Boran. In 1932 a bitter strike was opposed by an alliance of big house, parochial house and state and one of the longest disputes in Irish coal-mining history took place in 1944. Declining coal resources and prohibitive working costs heralded the end of Castlecomer's coal industry.

Castlecomer in the twentieth century has retained an equilibrium which is dependent on the migration of many of its younger people. It has maintained a manufacturing base in its textile and brick-making plant which utilises the fireclay on which the coal rested. Community development groups and central and local government have attempted to grapple with the endemic problem of unemployment and the town has evened out socially in this century. The other issue is the divide of religion, as obvious as in the last century. But the non-Catholic, mainly Church of Ireland, proportion in the town population is now just one per cent. As it gears itself for the future Castlecomer looks to its well-documented past, some of which has reposed uncatalogued in the National Library of Ireland since 1964. The basic form of the town is that planned by Anne, countess of Ormond. Bereft of coal, the Wandesfordes, and the big house (accidentally burned in 1966), the town has symbolically turned to the O'Brennans and last year descendants of famine emigrants from the town and hinterland participated in the first O'Brennan clan rally in Castlecomer.

**Select bibliography**
W. Tighe: *Statistical Survey of the County of Kilkenny*, Dublin, 1802
W. Nolan: *Fassadinin: Land, Settlement and Society in South-east Ireland, 1600-1850*, Dublin, 1979
T. Lyng: *Castlecomer Connections*, Castlecomer, 1984
A. Brennan and W. Nolan: 'Nixie Boran and the colliery community of north Kilkenny', in W. Nolan and K. Whelan (eds), *Kilkenny: History and Society*, Dublin, 1990, pp. 567-85

# BRAY

## Mary Davies

BRAY in County Wicklow is a town with a dual personality. Perhaps one could even say with a multi-layered personality, since its character has changed radically three times in the last 350 years. The spatial contrast can be appreciated by taking two views of the town. The first, looking southwards from a point on the esplanade near the railway station, is the classic view of a seaside resort: long terraces of Victorian hotels, boarding houses and villas, the promenade with its lawns and bandstand, brightly painted iron railings along the sea wall, and the curve of the beach leading on towards the prominent punctuation mark of Bray Head. This is the Bray created in the second half of the nineteenth century, the 'Brighton of Ireland'.

If the viewer stands instead some half a mile inland and looks southwards along Main Street, the impression is a quite different one. The scene here is that of a typical, bustling medium-sized town, that could be anywhere in Ireland. Two- and three-storey nineteenth-century buildings with shops at ground level follow a gentle rising curve towards the south-west and there is little to indicate the proximity of the Irish Sea.

Neither of these snapshots, however contrasting, takes us very far back in time: there are no ancient buildings in Bray to remind us of the distant past – no Early Christian round tower, no monastery ruins and no Anglo-Norman castle. And, as it happens, neither view takes in the old, almost forgotten, core of the settlement. To find this, it is necessary to step into a quiet backwater west of Main Street, close to the now deconsecrated St Paul's Church of Ireland church. Here, on a high bluff on the south side of the river, in about the year 1172, the Anglo-Norman knight Walter de Ridelisford chose the site for a castle in his newly-created manor of Bray. Like many others of its time, the castle served

*Bray, Breslin's Marine Hotel, c. 1858 (National Library of Ireland)*

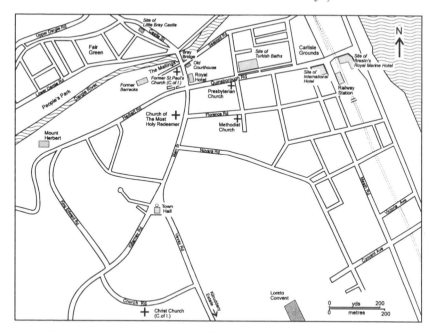

*Bray, based on Ordnance Survey of Ireland, six inches to one mile, 1937*

to protect the ford – the lowest crossing point of the Dargle River – which lay in the vicinity of the present Bray Bridge. Standing today in St Paul's churchyard, at a height of some sixty feet above the level of the river, one can visualise the panoramic view from de Ridelisford's strongpoint. Upstream the Dargle wandered across a marshy flood plain where the Lower Dargle Road and People's Park are today, with rolling countryside and hills beyond. Downstream the river widened into a muddy estuary as it discharged itself into the waters of the Irish Sea.

The exact site of de Ridelisford's castle is not now known. But a curve of ancient wall a few hundred yards west of the churchyard may be part of the bawn wall. St Paul's church itself, although seventeenth-century, is very probably on the site of the medieval church. The third building crucial to life in the medieval manor, the corn mill, lay below the castle on the river bank. A water-mill continued to operate on much the same site for some seven hundred years and the great complex of mill and brewery buildings that survived until recently on the Maltings was its descendant. As far as we know, this cluster of key buildings – castle, church and mill – with their attendant houses and cabins, was the earliest settlement near to the mouth of the Dargle River: the Vikings seem to have found little to interest them here, preferring Wicklow and Arklow, and the nearest Early Christian religious settlement of any size was probably that at Rathmichael, some three miles further north.

Although Bray soon held a weekly market and was also made a borough, there is little sign that the medieval settlement grew to be much more than a typical manorial village. One of its problems was that de Ridelisford had chosen the wrong side of the river. If the main threat of attack in the medieval period had come from the north, his castle would have been a well-positioned one, and Bray might have developed some strategic importance. But as it was the inhabitants of Bray must have spent the centuries looking over their shoulders towards the Wicklow Mountains, where the O'Tooles and the O'Byrnes presented a constant threat. Bray was burned in 1314, and it may have been after this set-back that the castle was rebuilt as a square, three-storey stone tower. It was still necessary in 1459 to build a new stone castle on the Dublin side of the Dargle to defend the ford from raiders coming from the south. This second castle, commemorated in Little Bray's Castle Street, survived into living memory. Had it not been destroyed in the late 1930s, it would have provided one memorial, at least, to Bray's precarious medieval past. The construction of this castle may also have marked the beginnings of settlement in Little Bray.

In the second half of the seventeenth century Bray began the first of its periods of dramatic change. As we stand at the viewpoint in St Paul's churchyard, two of the three main elements in this change are visible close at hand. The first, just below, is Bray Bridge, successor to the first stone bridge built over the Dargle in about 1660. The ford cannot have been an easy one to cross, with flash floods and high tides to contend with, and improved communications with Dublin helped Bray to develop as a market centre. The second element was an intangible legal one. Soon after the bridge was built 'the manor and lands of Great Bray' were formally partitioned between the second earl of Meath and the earl of Tyrconnell. Tyrconnell's share, which later became part of the Pembroke estate, was an elongated strip along the south side of the Dargle as far as Ballywaltrim, together with part of the area around St Paul's church. The earls of Meath, already based in Kilruddery, acquired the lion's share, including most of the area between the main street and the sea. This settlement of conflicting claims began a period of expansion for Bray, as each landlord granted leases for parcels of land around the town.

The third element is again a visible one. The plain rectangular building with a walled courtyard, still standing immediately west of the churchyard, is the military barracks, built in about 1700 and now divided into private houses. The presence of a military garrison in Bray throughout the eighteenth century was to provide a stimulus to trade and social life as well as an official pledge of protection in times of unrest.

Eighteenth-century Bray grew steadily as a market

centre, but it was still seen as a place at some remove from the sea. The town was not, however, entirely indifferent to the presence of this wider maritime world. The mouth of the Dargle provided a reasonably good harbour for the import of coal, timber and other necessities. At the other end of the shore, close to Bray Head, there was a small colony of fishermen who presumably relied upon Bray as a market for their catches. By and large, though, the seafront scene was still a rural one; green fields, a scattering of cottages along the shore and a rough track close to high water mark. The only road down to the sea was the ancestor of the present Seapoint Road, running from the vicinity of Bray Bridge to reach the shore near the present railway station.

But as the eighteenth century progressed, the first pre-figurations of Bray's future role as a resort began to appear. Two parallel movements began to affect the town. The first of these was the new interest in beautiful scenery. Here what had once been a disadvantage – Bray's proximity to the wild Wicklow Mountains – changed into a significant boon. When County Wicklow acquired the sobriquet 'the garden of Ireland', Bray became 'the gateway' to it. Just as Killarney became the base for touring the lakes and mountain passes of Kerry, so Bray became the starting point for tourists anxious to savour on foot, on horseback or by side-car the splendours of the Powerscourt waterfall, Dargle Glen, Lough Dan, Glendalough and the Glen of the Downs. In this the town was in some competition with its smaller neighbour, Enniskerry. But Bray was better served by road links with the Irish capital, particularly after 1800, and the town had a better infrastructure to attract the traveller.

It had, for instance, several good inns, of which the most famous and long-lasting was to be Mr Quin's. This hostelry, established in about 1770, survives to the present, greatly altered, as the Royal Hotel, which faces across the Main Street directly towards St Paul's. It was then conveniently next to the market place (where the old courthouse is now) as well as being on the main road from Dublin to Wicklow and Wexford. It was well known for its 'very superior accommodation'. Quin's Hotel was soon to benefit from the other great tourism development: the growing interest in sea bathing. At least one house was advertised for rent in Bray as early as the 1760s on the basis that it was 'convenient for sea bathing and goat's whey'. From the 1780s onwards there was a steady rise in the number of visitors who stayed in the hotel, rented a cottage or took lodgings in the area.

The consequent expansion of the Bray urban area from the mid-eighteenth century onwards is well charted on maps, beginning with two estate maps of the 1760s. At that time Bray was still very compact, with rows of houses confined to the area near the bridge and the neighbouring parts of Seapoint Road. St Paul's church and churchyard, the barracks and the two old castles (in Great Bray and Little Bray) were still the most prominent buildings. About half of the main street was still bounded by green fields and the only structure at its southern end, near the present town hall, was the pound. Over the next fifty years houses spread southwards up the street to reach this point and spill over into what are now the Killarney and Vevay Roads. By the time of the first ordnance survey maps in 1838, the view up Main Street from Quin's doorstep was not so very different from what it is today: Bray had become a substantial one-street town with a prominent Catholic church (built in 1824) on the site of the present Church of the Holy Redeemer, a Methodist chapel, and several schools. By now the Maltings area would have looked quite familiar too; the corn mill was an extensive structure and next to it was the equally impressive brewery. What the bystander of the 1830s would not have seen was any urban development seaward of Main Street. But there was already a portent. A long, straight ornamental avenue, planted with trees and shrubs, had been laid out from the main street area to the sea. This was 'Quin's Walk', planned by that enterprising hotelier to provide his guests with a gentle perambulation from the hotel to the seafront. It was to play a significant part in the changes to come.

Just as there are certain dates branded into the national consciousness, so the people of Bray have one date above all others engraved into theirs: 1854, the year of the coming of the railway. The extension of the Dublin–Kingstown (Dún Laoghaire) line as far as Bray in 1854 and subsequently to Wicklow and beyond had far-reaching repercussions for the town. Until then growth had been natural and haphazard – the earls of Meath had not tried to develop Bray as an estate town. But the Bray we see today owes the shape of most of the area between Main Street and the sea to consciously-made decisions, albeit largely uncoordinated ones. The concept of how the town should develop commercially was an overall consensus on the part of a small number of prominent people: it was to be a major 'up-market' holiday resort deliberately modelled on Brighton in England. The actual execution of this idea, though, proceeded in a piecemeal fashion, with different entrepreneurs and landlords each contributing a share.

The first factor to shape 'the Brighton of Ireland' was, of course, the positioning of the railway itself, immediately inland of the existing seafront cottages, leaving just sufficient land on the seaward side for new terraces of hotels and boarding houses. This was perhaps not ideal, with the necessary railway embankment cutting off most of the area under development from glimpses of the Irish Sea, but it was inevitable once the Dublin and Wicklow Railway Company had decided to blast a route around the cliffs of Bray Head. The siting of the railway station was the next most important factor. John Quin the elder struck an advantageous bargain with the railway company that was to have a profound effect on the shape of Bray. Quin was selling the company a vital stretch of seafront land, and the all-important railway station was sited at the east end of his 'Walk'. More than this, the railway company agreed to build a major new thoroughfare along the line of the Walk, to reach Main Street adjacent to Quin's Hotel. Quin is permanently commemorated in the name of this new road: Quinsborough Road. The date '1854' is on the building at its south-west corner.

The Quin family had therefore done all they could to ensure that their own establishment retained an advantageous position when the perimeter of Bray was suddenly extended eastwards to reach the seafront. They built a three-storey extension to the hotel, curving it elegantly round into Quinsborough Road, and before long the name was changed in keeping with Bray's new pretensions: it became the Royal Hotel. But the centre of gravity had shifted. If we start at the Main Street end of Quinsborough Road, we can move down to the railway station, the hub of Bray in the second half of the nineteenth century and the first part of the twentieth. And in this area development was shaped by men like William Dargan, already famous both as railway engineer and as organiser of the 1853 Industrial Exhibition in Dublin, his associate, Edward Breslin, and local builder John Brennan. Two major hotels sprang up within a few yards of the railway station: the International Hotel, then the largest in Ireland, on Quinsborough Road and Breslin's Royal Marine Hotel immediately seaward of the railway where the Bray market is held now. The International Hotel was built by John Brennan on a site acquired by Dargan. Dargan was also responsible for laying out the first esplanade (which he presented to the town), the elaborate but short-lived Turkish Baths (later the Assembly Rooms) and several handsome terraces of houses. We can no longer recapture the flavour of this area in its heyday. The fashionable hotels and the Turkish Baths have already gone and the Carlisle Grounds, once a notable venue for outdoor entertainment, are now scheduled for redevelopment.

If we wander along any of the roads near the seafront we will see the building development that took place from the 1850s onwards, as new roads criss-crossed the fields. Meath Road was laid out as a long straight avenue parallel to the seafront. Shorter avenues at right angles, Convent Avenue and Victoria Avenue, for instance, were run under the railway to reach the seafront. The substantial terraces of houses along Quinsborough Road and the esplanade were followed by less imposing ones along these other new streets. Early photographs taken from the slopes of Bray Head give the impression of a whole new town under construction.

This is a useful point at which to weigh Bray's advantages and disadvantages as a nineteenth-century seaside resort. The advantages start with the attractively curving bay with Bray Head behind, not unlike a mirror image of Llandudno in North Wales. The town had and has, as we have seen, the benefit of excellent scenery nearby in the Wicklow Mountains. These same mountains check the prevailing south-westerly winds so that rainfall is relatively low and the number of sunshine hours is high. And, like Brighton, Bray was seen as lying at a suitable distance from a capital city both to attract day visitors and holiday-makers and also to capture affluent commuters. What then were the disadvantages? One was the lack of a good sandy beach. Another was that Dublin, unlike the English capital, is itself adjacent to the sea and its citizens had no pressing need to travel as far afield as Bray to sample maritime pleasures. But the main problem was not so parochial. Ireland in the second half of the nineteenth century was recovering from the disastrous years of the great famine; any Irish holiday resort had serious economic disadvantages compared with those springing up across the water. The new British resorts depended upon the leisure and spending power, not just of the middle and upper classes, but of a great mass of urban wage-earners. No Irish resort could hope to attract the same crowds.

Valiant efforts were made. The town commissioners tried to keep up standards by introducing strict by-laws to keep the town tidy and orderly; they conducted a running battle with the Bray Head fishermen over inconvenience caused by their nets and fish catches, and with the car men who drove visitors into the Wicklow countryside over obstruction of the area around the railway station. The Bray Amusements Committee organised archery competitions, flower shows and firework displays in the Carlisle Grounds. There were boating regattas and polo matches. But there were no funds to build that most classic of seaside amenities, a pier, and plans for an electric tramway along the seafront and a railway line inland to Enniskerry were also abortive. The International Hotel had a chequered career and changed hands a number of times. By the turn of the century, after some fifty years of development, there were still empty building-lots dotted among the villas on most of the Victorian avenues.

This is not to say that Bray was not, in the Irish context, a successful resort. Certainly it attracted both holiday-makers and day trippers – 4,000 day trippers on one day alone at Easter 1861 for instance. The population doubled between 1851 and 1911 and the new permanent residents included many professional and business families with interests in Dublin as well as those attracted to Bray by the prospect of local work in the service industries. Nor was all the development in the seafront area. The Pembroke family made their contribution when the Honourable Sidney Herbert laid out Herbert Road, west of Main Street, in 1858-9 and built the impressive Mount Herbert. Other substantial houses in large grounds were also built out to the west and south-west. The 'top' end of the town was revitalised first by the construction of Christchurch, the elegant Church of Ireland church that superseded the old St Paul's, and then by the addition of the town hall, one of the Meath family's gifts to the town.

From 1900 onwards, growth was largely a matter of consolidation. Relatively modest housing filled in the gaps along Meath Road, Putland Road, Novara Avenue and neighbouring roads. Florence Road, first laid out in the 1850s, finally broke through into the main street to form a second line of access to the railway station. Breslin's Royal Marine Hotel, by this time more prosaically named the Station Hotel, was destroyed by fire in 1916 and replaced by the station buffet. The Royal Hotel, though, recovered from a period of eclipse as some of the predominance of the railway station area waned when motor transport began to compete with rail travel. This period came to an end in the late 1960s and early 1970s, when Bray underwent yet another transformation.

Seen from the 1990s, the ending of the holiday resort era in Bray seems as sudden as its start. This end is symbolised by the destruction by fire of the International Hotel in 1974 and the fact that it was not considered economic to rebuild it; the site, one of the most desirable in Bray a hundred years before, was to lie derelict for nearly twenty years until its recent redevelopment as a leisure centre. Bray's fortunes at this period were no different from those of its British counterparts; the traditional seaside resort declined with the rise of package holidays to the Mediterranean and the new freedom to move around offered by the motor car. Hotels lost business, boarding houses almost disappeared. But Bray has been vastly more fortunate than many resorts in Britain; the town has found new roles in the late twentieth century that will carry it through into the twenty-first. Boarding houses and villas have found a new use as nursing homes. Bray's proximity to Dublin has stood it in good stead and it has become a dormitory town, combining easy access to the capital by the Dart rapid rail service with lower land prices and fresher air. New housing estates now ring the old urban area, many of them in the grounds of the large late Victorian houses to the south-west and west. It has also developed its own manufacturing base, with factories on the Boghall estate at the southern end of the town and in Little Bray. Some of the resort ambience has survived and in summer the promenade and amusement arcades are thronged, as much with local residents as with visitors. The local film industry, based in Ardmore Studios, adds an international dimension. And the focus of the town has swung back to the geographical centre, so that the area at the junction of Main Street, Quinsborough Road and Herbert Road has regained its old place at the heart of things.

**Select bibliography**
G. D. Scott: *The Stones of Bray*, Dublin, 1913, facsimile reprint Bray, 1984
F. J. Seymour: *A Hundred Years of Bray and its Neighbourhood from 1770–1870 by an Old Inhabitant*, Dublin, 1907, facsimile reprint Blackrock, Co. Dublin, 1978
I. Moylan: *The Development and Growth of Bray, 1750–1900*, BA. dissertation, Department of History, Trinity College, Dublin, 1972
A. Flynn: *History of Bray*, Cork and Dublin, 1986
J. O'Sullivan, T. Dunne and S. Cannon (eds): *The Book of Bray*, Blackrock, Co. Dublin, 1989
K. M. Davies: 'For health and pleasure in the British fashion: Bray as a holiday resort, 1750–1914', M. Cronin and B. O'Connor (eds): *Tourism in Ireland: a Critical Analysis*, Cork, 1993, pp. 29-48

# SLIGO

## Mary O'Dowd

THE history of Sligo town has nearly always been something of an anomaly. Founded by the Normans in the thirteenth century, Sligo was the only Norman foundation in the north-west to flourish as a town. But when it did flourish as a town in the medieval period, it was under Gaelic not Norman rule. And this in itself is another unusual characteristic of Sligo's history: a town held by a Gaelic lord, the O'Connor Sligo, and with its own native Irish merchants – a very unusual phenomenon in Gaelic society, which was traditionally dominated by a rural economy with cattle as the main form of currency. Later, in the seventeenth century, Scottish settlers came to live and work in Sligo town. At that time, Sligo with its mixture of Irish and Scottish inhabitants must have looked very like a town in the Ulster plantation, despite the fact that this town is not in Ulster, but in Connacht. In the eighteenth and nineteenth centuries, Sligo continued to have a large Protestant population. English visitors to the west of Ireland often expressed their surprise at discovering Sligo's busy and hardworking inhabitants. The travellers usually attributed the prosperity of the town to the Scottish Protestant background of its inhabitants. Frank O'Connor put it slightly differently when he wrote of Sligo as the only civilised part of the western seaboard, although he was not prepared to commit himself on who civilised it.

So why did Sligo have such an unusual medieval history and why did its later history often have more in common with towns in Ulster than in other parts of Connacht? Well, one of the main reasons for Sligo's rather unusual history is its geographical position. It is situated on an important strategic site, on one of the main passages between the province of Connacht and the province of Ulster. It has always formed an important link between the two provinces. Long before the town was established, there was a bridge-

*Sligo in 1685 by Thomas Phillips (National Library of Ireland)*

head at Sligo which was much used by travellers passing from one province to the other. And the bridge continued to be important right through the history of the town. The town grew up around the bridge and, even today, its main focus is the river and its bridges. As Seán O'Faolain comments: 'every side street in Sligo seems to lead to a bridge.' The connecting or bridgehead role of Sligo between the provinces of Connacht and Ulster meant that it was never quite part of either province. And hence the history of Sligo is a mixture of traditions and developments in both provinces.

The Normans who founded the town in the thirteenth century were well aware of its bridgehead role. Maurice FitzGerald built Sligo castle beside the bridge and he hoped to use the castle to consolidate his control in north Connacht, and also to encroach on O'Donnell's territory lying to the north in Donegal. So FitzGerald planned to use the castle to establish control in both provinces. The FitzGeralds also made efforts to turn Sligo into something more than a military site. Apart from the castle they built a hospital which later became the site of St John's church. The FitzGeralds were also responsible for the founding of a Dominican friary, a little further up-river from the castle. The castle, abbey and hospital buildings formed the nucleus for the town.

The Norman dream of controlling the west of Ireland faded but their foundation of Sligo town survived. In the course of the Gaelic revival of the fourteenth century, the town was taken over by a branch of the O'Connor family who became known as the O'Connors Sligo. The O'Connors Sligo like their Norman predecessors recognised the strategic value of Sligo castle and used it as the centre of their lordship in north Connacht. But O'Connor control of Sligo was always hazardous. The town's military importance made it an attractive acquisition for neighbouring lords, particularly the O'Donnells of Donegal and the Burkes of Mayo and Galway. All these lords recognised that controlling Sligo castle would give them a dominating position in north Connacht. For much of the later middle ages, the castle was passed like a football between the O'Donnells and the Burkes, as one or other of these great lords gained the upper hand. The O'Connors were never powerful or strong enough to exercise independent control of Sligo.

Despite the military conflict of the fourteenth and fifteenth centuries, however, Sligo grew and its commercial life developed. The mid-fifteenth century seems to have been something of a boom time for Sligo. The good times were largely due to the fishing resources of the river and the neighbouring coast. Salmon in the river of Garvoge at Sligo and shoals of herring, which appeared off the west coast of Ireland at this time, attracted English and continental fishermen to Sligo and other west-coast ports. Rather than come with empty vessels to fish, the foreign fishermen brought with them goods which might prove attractive to locals in Sligo. And they found a ready market for their products, particularly for wine and salt, which was used to preserve fish and meat. It is from this time that the well-known rhyme dates:

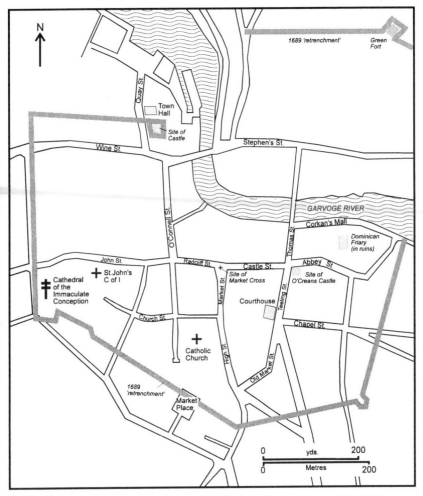

*Sligo, based on Ordnance Survey of Ireland, six inches to one mile, 1940, and Sligo City Development Plan 1992-1997*

Herring of Sligo and salmon of Bann
Have made in Bristol many a rich man.

As more commercial links were developed, the foreign traders took other goods from Sligo, apart from fish: cow hides and timber were among the most popular exports from the town.

The trade of Sligo was not entirely controlled by continental or English fishermen and merchants. Sligo also had its own native merchants, in the Crean family. The Creans were unusual, in the history of Gaelic Ireland, in that very few Gaelic Irish families earned their living by trading, as the Creans did. The family became wealthy enough to build large houses in the town, and to pay for impressive burial stones in the Dominican friary. Apart from the Creans, other Gaelic families in the Sligo area also shared in the commercial success of the town. The O'Connors Sligo, the O'Donnells, the Burkes and the MacDonaghs all claimed a share in the customs of Sligo. All of which belies the image of Gaelic Ireland as a rural society whose chiefs had no business acumen or interest in commercial enterprise. The profits of the town must have been an important part of the economic life of the surrounding region.

The prosperity that the boom time of the fifteenth century brought to Sligo led to the town's expansion. Houses for local merchants such as the Creans were built between the castle and the abbey where Castle Street is today. The street owes its name to the fact that the merchants' houses resembled castles or tower-houses similar to those which still survive in Galway. Other buildings in Sligo town such as the abbey were also repaired and renovated in the late fifteenth century.

The prosperity of Sligo did not survive into the sixteenth century. The shoals of herring disappeared and the number of foreign fishermen coming to trade in the area declined. The Crean family continued to do business in the town but the wars of the sixteenth century made commercial life difficult. In the rebellion of the northern chiefs at the end of the century, Sligo suffered badly. Once again, its strategic importance became significant as both O'Donnell and the Tudor administration tried to seize control of it. In the end, O'Donnell, rather than let the English army gain control of the castle, destroyed the town. O'Donnell's destruction of Sligo at the end of the sixteenth century marked, rather ignobly, the end of the Gaelic phase of Sligo's history.

The seventeenth century marked a new era in the town's history, an era which might be described as its Scottish phase. For the most remarkable thing about Sligo in the seventeenth century is the large number of British settlers living in the town. Many of the settlers had Scottish surnames. They set up shops and brought new skills to the town. They included general merchants, clothiers, shoemakers, cutlers and butchers.

Mixed in among the Scottish settlers were a number of English families, often originating with Elizabethan soldiers who had stayed on in Sligo after the wars of the sixteenth century. A prominent inhabitant of the town at this time was Roger Jones. Jones had come to Ireland as a soldier, frcm Derbyshire. He settled in Sligo after the war, and built a large house in the town. He also had a shop in the town and traded in wool. Jones was also involved in receiving land in mortgage, lending money to impoverished Irish landowners in return for a mortgage on their land. The money was rarely repaid and in this way Jones acquired possession of the mortgaged property. With this shop, money-lending and trading in wool, Jones was the precursor of the gombeen man who became such a familiar figure in small Irish towns in the nineteenth century.

We know very little about the origins of the Scottish settlers who came to Sligo in the early seventeenth century but it is likely that they first came to Ireland with a view to settling in the Ulster plantation. Some of them may even have been recruited by Ulster landlords, to settle on Ulster estates, possibly in the north-west. One can imagine Scottish families arriving in remote parts of Donegal or Fermanagh and looking around them with despair and fear at the isolation and barrenness of their new homes. Some may have decided to look elsewhere, moving southwards or westwards towards the sea. Sligo, as an existing port, may have offered better prospects for a new life than the hills or lakes of Donegal or Fermanagh. And so these Scottish families settled down in Sligo.

We don't have many statistics about population for the town in the early seventeenth century but there may have been as many as 250–300 people of British origin in Sligo before 1641. Given that the total population of the town was probably no more than 500 people, the British population may have been in the majority. These figures may seem surprisingly low, but Sligo's population compares favourably with other Irish towns; and was considerably larger than most towns (incorporated boroughs) in the Ulster plantation where the average population was less than 200. In other words, Sligo in the early seventeenth century was a more successfully planted town than many of the towns in the Ulster plantation.

A crucial question, of course, is how did the new settlers get on with their Irish neighbours? There is certainly evidence to suggest that newcomer and native could do business together and the business enterprises of the newcomers in the town depended, to a large extent, on the patronage and custom of the Irish. But doing business together and carrying on polite conversation are not always an indication of a truly integrated community, as we know only too well today from the history of Northern Ireland. And the outbreak of the rebellion in 1641 revealed that all was not well in the urban community of Sligo. Like other parts of Ireland, this district had its share of the horrors of the 1640s. Early in January 1642, many of the British settlers in the town were rounded up and put into the town jail. Later the same night they were attacked by a group of local men and many of them were killed. After the massacre, most of the remaining settlers in the town left Sligo, often fleeing to what they saw as the safer environment of Ulster. The massacre in Sligo jail was a product of the general atmosphere in Ireland at the time. But in the immediate context of the urban community the massacre also reflected underlying tensions in society between the newcomers and the local population.

But whatever the cause of the massacre, it did not deter British settlers from coming to live in Sligo, after the ending of the wars of the 1640s. In the 1650s and 1660s, there was a considerable increase in the number of new British settlers and again many of them had Scottish surnames. Rough population figures suggest that there were about 200 British families in Sligo town by 1680 and about 100–150 Irish families. So, again, the majority of Sligo's inhabitants in the late seventeenth century may have been Protestant. The Sligo British community was a mixture of older settlers who had returned after the war, and soldiers who had served in the wars of the 1640s and had decided to settle in the area. Other settlers were still serving as soldiers, because late seventeenth-century Sligo was a garrison town. The commonwealth government, like many military commanders before them, recognised the strategic value of Sligo and built two forts in the town. One called the Stone or New Fort was built on the site of the old medieval castle near the river and bridge, close to where the town hall now stands. The second fort, known as the Green or Sod Fort, was placed on a hill to the north of the town. The soldiers serving in the forts lived in houses and cabins in the vicinity.

So many of the settlers in Sligo in the second half of the seventeenth century were serving or ex-soldiers. But there were also merchant families living and trading in the town. We know, for example, that the old Gaelic family of Crean were still an important business family in the town. They were joined by other merchant families with Scottish surnames such as Gamble, Braxton, Johnston and Delap. Also working and living in Sligo at this time were families related to Galway merchant families such as the Frenches, Darcys and Lynches. The Galway families and the Creans were Catholics but this does not seem to have prevented them from trading and working in Sligo in the second half of the seventeenth century.

Sligo was never a large trading centre but it served as a market centre and distribution centre for the north-west and developed in the course of the seventeenth century a reputation for having a good market, particularly in livestock. The increase in population in the seventeenth century also led to an expansion in the buildings and layout of the town. By the 1680s, a street pattern had been developed. Sligo was never a planned town and, as in medieval times, the only clear centre in the town was the river-crossing. The main streets ran parallel to the river. The most fashionable streets were Castle Street and Radcliffe Street (later renamed Grattan Street). Radcliffe Street was called after Sir George Radcliffe who had bought a large portion of the town from the O'Connor Sligo family in the 1630s. High Street, running southwards from Radcliffe Street, had also been established by the 1680s. Near High Street was a new market place. Old Market Street, the site of the old medieval market, had already been named by the 1680s. The development of a new and presumably bigger market place by the 1680s is a reflection of the success of Sligo as a market centre. St John's church marked the most westerly point of the town while the Dominican friary lay on the eastern border. Bridge Street (now O'Connell Street) connected Castle and Radcliffe Streets with the Stone Fort on the quay and also led to the bridge near the fort. On the northern side of the river, Stephen's Street had been formed and it too ran parallel to the river. On the hill behind Stephen Street were the town gallows and the Green Fort. A new bridge connected Stephen Street with the abbey and Castle Street on the southern side of the river.

Catholic and Protestant merchants lived side by side in Castle and Radcliffe Streets and, as in the early seventeenth century, they seemed to do business together. But this did not prevent them taking different sides in the wars at the end of the seventeenth century. The Catholic merchants identified with the cause of James II while their Protestant neighbours supported William, and joined up with other northern towns in his defence. The defeat of James also sealed the fate of the Catholic merchants in the town. Most of them disappear after this time. In the eighteenth century the town was firmly in the control of the Protestant merchant class.

And throughout the eighteenth century, Sligo remained a town with a large Protestant population. Of a total population of about 3,000 in 1749, almost half were Protestant. The town continued also to have much in common with towns in the north of Ireland. It shared in the prosperity brought to Ulster through the expansion in the linen industry in the second half of the eighteenth century. Sligo became an export centre for linen and in 1760 a linen hall was established in the town.

Religious developments in the town also reflected an Ulster pattern rather than a Connacht one. Methodism, for example, which won so many converts in the north of Ireland, was also popular in Sligo; and John Wesley was pleased with the large congregations which he attracted when he visited the town on many occasions in the second half of the eighteenth century.

The linen industry brought prosperity to Sligo but the industry declined rather dramatically in the early nineteenth century. This was not a good time for Sligo. Famine in the 1820s, followed by a cholera epidemic in 1832 and the great famine in 1846, greatly reduced the population of the town. The cholera epidemic in particular caused widespread suffering and death in Sligo.

It was not until the second half of the nineteenth century that an air of prosperity returned to the town and Sligo began to grow to the size it is today. Improvements in transport technology by sea, and later by rail, helped the town expand. The introduction of steamships contributed much to the development of Sligo's overseas trade. One of the most important steam shipping companies was that owned by the Middleton and Pollexfen families, the Pollexfens being the family of Jack and William Butler Yeats's mother, Susan. Their company ran steamships between Sligo, Liverpool, Glasgow, Derry and further afield. The steamships enabled Sligo to become part of a wider trading market. The railway reached the town in 1862 and it too helped to develop the commercial life of Sligo. The prosperity of the town was reflected in the many new buildings which appeared in Sligo at this time. The town hall was built in the 1860s, the new assize courts in the 1870s and the Bank of Ireland and the Ulster Bank also built new premises in the town.

The Yeats brothers, William and Jack, poet and artist, depicted in their art the excitement and bustle of Sligo quays in the late nineteenth century. William wrote fondly of childhood days spent at the quays where he gazed with wonder and admiration at the foreign sailors wearing earrings. All his dreams, he remembered, were of ships and one of his earliest memories was of a much-treasured toy boat. The poet envied the ability of his brother Jack to recapture in paint their youthful memories of ships and fishing on the quays.

But although the two brothers had good childhood memories of Sligo, William Butler Yeats also depicted the rather claustrophobic and inward-looking atmosphere of the Protestant merchant families in the town. Looked down on, socially, by local Protestant landed families, such as the Gore-Booths in Lissadell or the Coopers in Markree, the Sligo merchant families felt increasingly under threat from the Catholics of the town. Yeats wrote of his family circle where everyone 'despised nationalists and Catholics' and the young poet wanted to die fighting Fenians. He also wrote of first learning the pleasure of rhyme from a book of Orange verse, which he read with the stable boy employed in his grandfather's house.

The fears of business families such as the Middletons and Pollexfens are understandable. In many parts of Ireland in the late nineteenth century, the Catholic middle class were encroaching on Protestant power. Given the large Protestant population in Sligo this was a more painful process there than in many other parts of Ireland. Everywhere in the town in the nineteenth century there were signs of increasing Catholic prosperity and confidence. Many of the new buildings in the town were associated with the Catholic church: a new Dominican friary built in 1846, a Sisters of Mercy convent established in 1846, an Ursuline convent built in 1850, a new Catholic cathedral built in 1874, a seminary college opened in 1880, and by the 1890s the Christian Brothers had also arrived in Sligo. And as the town moved into the twentieth century street-names were changed to reflect the new heroes. Thus Radcliffe Street became Grattan Street, Knox's Street became O'Connell Street, Albert Street became Teeling Street and Victoria Road, Markieviecz Road.

But despite the growth of Catholic power, the Protestant tradition of Sligo remained strong into the twentieth century. And it gave Sligo town its unique blend of cultures and traditions which so many modern Irish writers and artists have found so attractive.

**Select bibliography**
W. G. Wood-Martin: *The History of Sligo County and Town from the Earliest Ages to the Present Time*, 3 vols, Dublin, 1882-97
T. O'Rorke: *History of Sligo, Town and County*, 2 vols, Dublin, 1989
J. G. Simms: 'Sligo in the Jacobite war, 1689-91', *Irish Sword*, vii (1965), pp. 14-30
D. A. Gillmor: 'The development of Sligo as a regional capital', *Geographical Viewpoint*, i (1967), pp 191-200
A. Thomas: 'Sligo', *The Walled Towns of Ireland*, ii, Dublin, 1992, pp. 238-9

# ATHLONE

## Harman Murtagh

THE overriding reason for Athlone's emergence as a sizeable town in the great damp lowland plain of Ireland is its location at a shallow point on the River Shannon, to which esker ridges, running across the surrounding bogs and wetlands, provide convenient access from both east and west, just north of the Dublin-Galway axis. The river crossing explains the name Athlone – Áth Luain in Irish, meaning Luan's ford – which has been in use for over a thousand years.

The town was created, and has been sustained, by the focus of traffic on the river crossing, and its consequent strategic and therefore military importance. This provided the conditions and security in which markets, fairs, commerce, industry, settlement and the development of urban institutions could occur. The immediate approaches to the river crossing have largely dictated the plan of the town core. Athlone's growth has tended to be along the eskers which carry the east-west thoroughfare, with the result that the town has a linear layout and a straggly unplanned appearance. Although its hinterland is not agriculturally rich, the townsmen have long exploited the neighbouring bogs, sandhills, meadows and fisheries. The river itself has been an artery of communication between the midlands and west Munster. But it has also divided Athlone into two towns, which for most of their history have been in different parishes, dioceses, counties and even provinces.

Athlone has never been the site of a scientific archaeological excavation. However, almost a hundred prehistoric objects have been found, mainly on the river bed. These indicate that the ford was of importance in the neolithic and bronze ages. The first evidence for actual settlement is provided by five grave slabs, thought to date from the mid-eighth to eleventh centuries, which suggest an unrecorded church site on the east river bank. Two Viking arm-rings are a

*Athlone Castle in 1843 by F. W. Fairholt (Mr and Mrs S. C. Hall,* Ireland: its Scenery, Character, *etc.*)

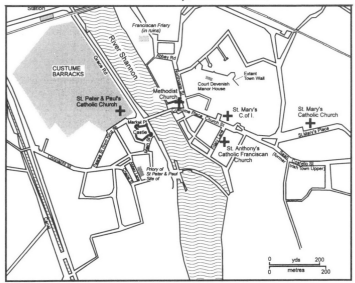

*Athlone, based on Ordnance Survey of Ireland, six inches to one mile, 1952*

reminder that Norse fleets were active on the mid-Shannon in the ninth and tenth centuries.

Documentary sources indicate that settlement at Athlone intensified in the twelfth century. In 1120 Toirrdelbach Ó Conchobair, the expansionist king of Connacht, erected what was probably the first bridge to facilitate his incursions into Meath. Five successive wicker or wooden bridges, built by the Ó Conchobairs, followed in the next forty years, all being demolished by the kings of Meath. Norman bridges, including one of stone, are mentioned in the thirteenth century, but only ferries after 1306. No subsequent bridge appears to have existed until 1567 when a new stone bridge of nine arches was completed on the instructions of Queen Elizabeth's Irish lord deputy, Sir Henry Sidney. Later, he aptly described it as 'a piece found serviceable, I am sure durable it is, and I think memorable'.

Sidney's bridge was the focus of much of the action during the great siege of 1691, the most dramatic event in Athlone's history. It involved the resistance of the Irish Jacobites to the attempt by the 20,000-strong multinational army of William of Orange to break into Connacht. Ironically, the Williamites eventually crossed the river by means of the old ford. In the 1840s Sidney's bridge was replaced by the present town bridge erected by the Shannon commissioners. A second bridge, approached by a new relief road, was opened in 1991.

Toirrdelbach Ó Conchobair also built a wooden castle at Athlone in 1129. Possibly it is identifiable with the later 'house' of his son, Ruaidrí, and with the *bodún* occupied by the Normans before 1200. Alternatively, the latter may have been the bailey of a motte. The precise location of any of these twelfth-century structures is unknown. One view is that a motte may form the core of the present stone castle, erected by the Normans on the west river bank. The first phase of its construction was the central free-standing polygonal tower, completed in 1210 and still extant, although much rebuilt. The curtain wall and three-quarter round towers were added in the 1270s. For most of its history, Athlone Castle has been a government stronghold and while the residence of the presidents of Connacht it was an important administrative centre. Its present appearance and atmosphere owe much to its remodelling as a platform for artillery during the Napoleonic wars, and its use as an annexe of the neighbouring military barracks. It has recently been refurbished, and now contains a small museum and a visitor centre in which Athlone's history is highlighted by means of an impressive audio-visual presentation.

A town wall was apparently built in the thirteenth century, but was in ruins by Tudor times, when new east and north gatehouses were erected in the Leinster town. Their location is recalled by the street-names Northgate Street and Dublin Gate Street. A stone curtain was added in the 1630s, at the townsmen's expense. The Cromwellian government strengthened the wall and the east gate with four stone bastions. These were four-sided defence works which projected from the main rampart. In the eighteenth century the east gate was demolished and the Dublin road pushed through the salient of its protective bastion. Prior to that, the exit was via the narrow sharp-angled lane nearby, known still as The Bawn from its proximity to the open space enclosed by the bastion. The north gate was removed in 1840. A substantial portion of the Leinster town wall and its bastions survives, albeit ivy-covered and rather neglected. The street-name Bastion Street is a reminder that the Connacht town was fortified in the 1650s with earthen ramparts, of which nothing now remains. Prior to that, security west of the river had depended on the castle and a defensive ditch. Early military engineers were concerned at the domination of the Connacht town by the adjoining esker. The result was the construction there in the early nineteenth century of a major artillery defence system, now obliterated by the housing scheme known as Battery Heights, a name which recalls the former function of the site.

The extensive military barracks, which today is the headquarters of the Irish army's western command, has evolved from temporary accommodation for soldiers, constructed amidst the ruins of the Connacht town in the wake of the siege of 1691. Its modern name, Custume Barracks, commemorates an Irish hero of that encounter. The earliest extant structures, a cavalry barrack and a riding house, are thought to date from *c.* 1700; and located around its spacious squares is a well-maintained collection of Georgian, Victorian and modern buildings. The tradition of military life is strong in Athlone, and soldiers have always taken a prominent role in the town's sporting, cultural, philanthropic and social activities.

In the west town the earliest documented religious foundation was the Cluniac priory of Saints Peter and Paul, a product of the twelfth-century reform movement, located in the Connacht town in the vicinity of Abbey Lane. No remains are extant, but at the dissolution it comprised a church of nave and single transept, with a tower, cloister and conventual buildings. A penal chapel is mentioned near the suburb of Bellaugh in 1719, and a T-shaped Roman Catholic parish church, with interior galleries, was erected in Chapel Street in 1797. This was superseded by the Italianate church at the Market Place, west of the town bridge, opened in 1937, and sufficiently imposing to be regularly mistaken for a cathedral. The priory patrons remain those of the parish which is in the diocese of Elphin. An independent Church of Ireland parish only functioned in the west town from 1802 to 1941. The former parish church, off Ganly Place, is now a centre of the society of St Pius X for the celebration of the traditional Latin mass.

East Athlone was the site of one of the first Franciscan houses in Ireland, founded *c.* 1240. No remains are extant, but the friary appears to have been located near the river, and an associated foundation may have been a spittal house, or leper hospital, in Mardyke Street. The Franciscans have maintained a remarkable continuity of presence in Athlone or its vicinity. The roofless friary at Abbey Road is a product of the short-lived Catholic revival of the 1680s. The present Hiberno-Romanesque church at Friary Lane, completed in 1931, is the fourth, since the mid-eighteenth century, to occupy the site. In the fifteenth century a separate vicarage dedicated to St Mary, also the friary patroness, was established for east Athlone and its environs. The area corresponded to the tribal territory of the indigenous Ó Breens. The medieval parish church was located in the vicinity of the present Church of Ireland church in Church Street. Although this is a nineteenth-century structure, the taller of its two towers is a remnant of the seventeenth-century successor to the medieval church. St Mary's was in the diocese that bore the proud name of Clonmacnoise, but which was in fact too small and poor to be viable. After the reformation it was united to Meath in the Church of Ireland, and in the eighteenth century to the Roman Catholic diocese of Ardagh. Chapel Lane off Sean Costello Street, the former Leinster Irishtown, was the site of a mid-eighteenth-century penal chapel, replaced in 1795 by a T-shaped Roman Catholic church, more prominently located at Gleeson Street. This, in turn, was succeeded in 1861 by the present dignified Gothic-revival structure at St Mary's Place.

Religious nonconformity was represented at Athlone by Anabaptists and Quakers in the seventeenth century, and subsequently by Presbyterians, Baptists and Methodists. The Wesleyan church in Northgate Street is an attractive Gothic-revival building dating from 1865. The decline of the Protestant population in the twentieth century has led to the closure of the Presbyterian church on the riverside and the Baptist chapel at St Mary's Place. Both buildings have now been converted to commercial use.

The earliest recorded schools date from the seventeenth century. Subsequently there were a large number of private academies, usually short-lived. However, classical and English schools established c. 1700 lasted until the nineteenth century, and the Ranelagh Endowed School from 1764 to 1936. Its purpose-built school-house, designed by John Ensor, was demolished in 1991. A Church of Ireland primary school has been in existence since 1826. Roman Catholic national and secondary schools were developed in both parishes in the nineteenth century, generally by, or in association with, religious orders. Of the premises occupied by the religious, the Bower convent in particular is a splendidly sited, cut-stone building, with a modern wing and boarding school. Third-level education was introduced in 1970 with the opening of a regional technical college. This institution has a current enrolment of approximately 2,500 students.

Athlone's strategic importance and commercial potential combined to ensure that by the early thirteenth century the town on both sides of the river, with the castle, was owned by the king. After the dissolution, the extensive property of the Cluniac priory was added to the royal estate, which was assigned to the support of the presidents of Connacht. On the abolition of the provincial administration, the estate passed to the first earl of Ranelagh, a favourite and financier of King Charles II, and was left by him for the support of free schools. Except where the freehold has been acquired by the tenants, the estate remains vested in the educational charity known as the Incorporated Society for Promoting Protestant Schools in Ireland. In general, the interest of these various proprietors in Athlone was financial, and only rarely did they devote attention or resources to the town's physical development.

Burgesses are mentioned in the thirteenth century, although the earliest known charter dates only from 1599. It was superseded by a second charter of 1606 which established a corporation comprising a sovereign, burgesses and freemen. This body functioned until 1840 when it was dissolved and replaced by municipal commissioners, and later by an urban district council. In 1899 the Connacht town was transferred from Roscommon to County Westmeath. Athlone was a parliamentary borough from 1606 to 1885. The original corporation boundary was defined as 'the whole circuit and extent of land and water, lying within a compass of a mile and a half from the middle of the bridge'. This extensive space was greatly reduced in the nineteenth century and today the built-up area spills across the urban boundary in several directions. A proposal to extend the boundary into Westmeath is currently under consideration, but there appears to be no parallel move to include the suburbs to the west which are in south Roscommon.

The growth of Athlone has been steady, if unspectacular. In 1620 its population was about 1,300; by 1832, it was over 6,000; and in 1986 the built-up area had almost 16,000 people, making it the largest inland town in the state after Kilkenny. However, its position in the league-table of Irish towns has often fluctuated. It seems to have been relatively important and prosperous in the twelfth and thirteenth centuries, in the mid-sixteenth to mid-seventeenth centuries, and in the latter half of the nineteenth century. The late middle ages and the eighteenth and early nineteenth centuries were amongst the low points.

Fairs and markets are mentioned from the 1220s, and a market house was erected before 1600 in what is now Custume Place. There were fair greens, pounds and market places on both sides of the Shannon. The thoroughfares leading down to Sidney's bridge, the present Main Street and Church Street, were known at one time, respectively, as Connaught and Leinster Market Streets. The establishment of a 'right good' weekly stage-coach service between Dublin and Athlone followed the introduction of toll roads in the 1730s. The best-known of several eighteenth-century inns was the Three Blackamoors' Heads in what is now Main Street. Haire's Royal Hotel opened in Mardyke Street in 1809 and today, in modernised premises, continues to trade as the Royal Hoey Hotel. Rourke's Hotel, in Church Street, is now the Prince of Wales, a change of name adopted in 1863. Some of these establishments had stables attached, and elsewhere there were independent stables such as those maintained in Mardyke Street in the 1840s for Charles Bianconi's passenger cars. As early as the mid-eighteenth century Athlone had its own short-lived bank. Today, all the leading commercial banks are represented in the town, and the Allied Irish Bank still occupies the handsome stone building at the east end of the bridge, purpose-built for the Provincial Bank in the 1850s. Opposite, the Ritz Cinema, designed by Michael Scott, is an uncompromisingly modern structure in concrete and glass, never completed as originally conceived, and sadly now scheduled for demolition. A shambles district for the slaughter and sale of meat was situated at the south end of the Connacht town near the river, which was convenient for the downstream disposal of offal.

In the early seventeenth century there were about two

hundred houses in Athlone. At that time, as part of an arrangement which gave the townsmen secure titles to their properties, they agreed to build 'houses of brick and stone after the English manner'. Of those erected, the finest was Court Devenish, a large U-shaped house with stone-mullioned windows. Much of its facade still survives in a private garden in the centre of the Leinster town. The solid two- and three-storey business premises of the middle class were built along the commercial streets leading to the bridge, with their residences alongside or overhead. Fry Place, named after its developer, is a handsome Georgian terrace dating from 1806. Lanes of smaller houses and cottages were sometimes developed on the long plots to the rear of the larger premises. Eighty per cent of the 960 houses in Athlone in 1861 were reckoned to be of the first or second class, that is to say with five or more rooms and windows.

Beyond the town centre, both east and west of the river, were warrens of single-storey cottages with, nearby, the ominously-named Gallows Hills, not that there is any record of these being actually employed as places of execution. In the seventeenth century the whole west town was referred to as Irishtown. Later, this term was used for the east-town cottage suburb adjacent to the Dublin road. Today, the cottages are gone, having been supplanted this century by 1,200 local-authority houses, grouped in rather drab estates which bear the names of saints and patriots. Garden Vale and Goldsmith Terrace are attractive brick-built terraces of middle-class houses dating from the 1890s. A handful of detached villas, such as Annesfield, New Court, Montree and Mount View, were built beyond the urban perimeter in the nineteenth century. These have now become part of the suburbs which have expanded to cater for the car-owning middle class, who no longer reside in the town centre.

Partly because it has never been a cathedral or county town, Athlone is rather lacking in architectural distinction. However, the lock, dam, town bridge and riverside quays, all in cut limestone, are an impressive and handsome monument to the skills of their Victorian engineers. Their completion had the practical effect of opening the Shannon to navigation through Athlone for the first time, thereby making redundant the by-pass canal constructed in the eighteenth century on the west side of the town. For a period Athlone became an inland port of some importance, with passenger boats docking and a crane unloading cargo from barges into warehouses on the quays. The development of more rapid road and rail transport finally ended commercial traffic on the Shannon in the 1950s. Today, the magnificent riverside facilities are entirely given over to pleasure boating, which itself has become a significant commercial activity linked to tourism.

The fast flow of the river, prior to the construction of the navigation works, powered medieval flour mills and later a number which were constructed on Sidney's bridge. Georgian Athlone had a national reputation, acknowledged by both Jonathan Swift and George Berkeley, for the manufacture of felt hats. Brewing, distilling and linen manufacturing were significant industries in the eighteenth and early nineteenth centuries. There were also a number of small manufacturing businesses aimed at meeting specific local needs, such as salt-processing, soap-boiling, boat-building and a brickworks.

Athlone became an important railway centre from 1851, with the arrival of the Midland Great Western Railway which linked it to Dublin, via Mullingar, and subsequently to Galway. An imposing iron viaduct carried the railway across the Shannon where a fine station, to the design of J. S. Mulvany, was erected close to the west bank. The Great Southern and Western Railway followed in 1859, linking Athlone to the Dublin–Cork line at Portarlington. Its station in the east town, after a period of dereliction, has been restored as the town's only railway station since 1985. Engine sheds, goods stores and cattle pens were constructed. The Great Northern and Western Railway linked Athlone to Castlebar after 1860.

The railways attracted modern industry. A steam sawmill and joinery works in the west town employed up to two hundred hands. Athlone Woollen Mills opened in 1859 and by the end of the century supported a labour force of four hundred, and had an output of 16,000 yards of cloth per week. Its premises beside the river were largely destroyed by fire in 1940. The textile tradition was maintained by the cotton-manufacturing firm of Gentex, situated at the old Ranelagh school premises. It became the major industry of the mid-twentieth century, only finally ceasing production in the 1980s. By then, fortunately, American and Scandinavian interests had established a number of new, high-technology industries in industrial estates on the town's periphery. These firms continue to prosper and expand, and they provide significant employment.

The latter half of the nineteenth century saw major improvements in the provision of utilities and other public services. Constabulary barracks, dispensaries, gas works and post offices were established in both the east and west towns. A workhouse, to the standard design of the board of works architect, George Wilkinson, with accommodation for nine hundred paupers, was built at Abbey Road, together with a fever hospital, now superseded by a modern district hospital and health centre. A new courthouse, street-lighting, piped sewage, a waterworks, asphalt footpaths, a volunteer fire brigade and street name-plates were all in place before 1900. The twentieth century has added a new town hall and government buildings, including accommodation for a section of the Department of Education, asphalt streets, a state-of-the-art waste disposal facility, and of course electricity and telephones. A modern sewage treatment works is nearing completion.

When the town bridge was re-sited in the nineteenth century, traffic to the west was diverted along Grace Road, which was newly constructed at the time between the military barracks and the river. This had the effect of by-passing most of the Connacht town which gradually declined into a commercial backwater. Henceforth, business life focused increasingly on the Leinster town where Church Street, Mardyke Street and Sean Costello Street, which together form the route from the bridge to the Dublin Road, acquired the popular epithet 'the golden mile'. In recent years, even on this thoroughfare, there has been a diminution of commerce, for reasons that include traffic congestion, parking difficulties and urban sprawl. Trade has leaked to suburban shops and supermarkets, to other midland towns, and to Dublin and Galway.

The completion in 1991 of the new Shannon bridge and six-mile relief road on the northern perimeter of the built-up area was a major development which reminds us of the essence of Athlone's existence. Undoubtedly it will benefit the town as a whole and ensure its future. However, very extensive resources of planning, capital and enterprise will be needed to consolidate the economy of the old town in the face of the challenge posed by the new relief road.

**Select bibliography**
G. T. Stokes: 'Athlone in the seventeenth century', *Journal of the Royal Society of Antiquaries of Ireland*, xxi (1890), pp. 198-215
M. K. Hanley: *The Story of Custume Barracks, Athlone, 1697–1974*, Athlone, 1974
*Journal of the Old Athlone Society*, 1969-
M. Keany and G. O'Brien (eds): *Athlone Bridging the Centuries*, Mullingar, 1991
H. Murtagh: *Irish Midland Studies: Essays in Commemoration of N. W. English*, Athlone, 1980
H. Murtagh: 'Athlone', *Irish Historic Towns Atlas*, no. 6, Royal Irish Academy, Dublin, 1994
G. O'Brien: *St Mary's Parish, Athlone: an History*, Longford, 1989

# DUNGARVAN

## L. J. Proudfoot

'CROWDED with miserable houses, irregular in appearance, ... Dungarvan deserved the reproachful epithets which travellers universally bestowed upon it. There were no regular market places, no public water works; the courthouse was considered unsafe ... [and] there was no bridge, and consequently no way of passing from the town to the Waterford side of the river, except by ferry boat.' So wrote the Rev. R. H. Ryland in 1824, describing the condition of Dungarvan sixty years earlier in 1764. Ryland then went on to describe, in glowing terms, the numerous improvements in the town which the duke of Devonshire, who then owned much of it, had paid for since the turn of the century.

Walking through the town today, much remains to be seen of the duke's improvements, but also something too of the earlier town which existed long before them. The relative prosperity of recent years has left its mark in the industries and a new by-pass on the outskirts of Dungarvan but has left the historic core of the town largely untouched. Thus as in so many of Ireland's historic towns, we can trace much of the unfolding story of Dungarvan's growth and changing fortunes from the streets and buildings which exist in the centre of the town today. In particular, Dungarvan illustrates characteristic aspects of two of the main periods of urban development in Ireland: the widespread Anglo-Norman town foundations of the thirteenth century; and the even more numerous attempts by landlords to establish or improve towns and villages on their estates in the eighteenth and early nineteenth centuries.

Although Dungarvan has traditionally been supposed to have grown up around an Augustinian monastery founded by St Garvin in the seventh century, there is no firm historical evidence for this. St Garvin's monastery was known as Achadh Garbhain. Earlier writers have assumed that the

*Shop-fronts in Dungarvan*

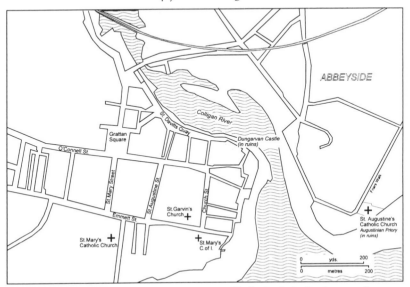

*Dungarvan, based on Ordnance Survey of Ireland, six inches to one mile, 1922-3*

similarity between the monastery's name and that of the modern town indicated that the one grew out of the other. This may have been so – something similar certainly happened elsewhere in Ireland, for example at Kells in County Meath and at Armagh – but at Dungarvan we do not know for certain that this was the case. For the present, therefore, we must conclude that the thread of urban life probably began in Dungarvan with the arrival of the Anglo-Norman colonists sometime around 1175. Their first act was to build a series of castles to subdue the district. The remains of the first of these – a simple earthen motte and bailey – survive at Gallowshill to the west of the modern town. This may have formed part of the western defences of the lands retained by the Normans in County Waterford following the treaty of Windsor in 1175. Shortly afterwards, possibly in 1185 at the command of Henry II's son John – the lord of Ireland – work started on its replacement. A substantial stone castle was built to command the natural harbour at the mouth of the Colligan River. By 1209 this was complete. Though much altered in later centuries before being partly destroyed by the Irish Republican Army in 1922, its remains still stand today at the mouth of the harbour on the end of Davitt's Quay.

The medieval town of Dungarvan grew up in the shadow of this castle and under its protection. The town seems to have gained an early importance in the Norman colony as the administrative centre of the royal manor of Dungarvan. The 'province' of Dungarvan had been surrendered to King John by Donald Uffeld in 1204, and remained in the King's personal possession until 1215. In that year he granted custody of the castle and vill of Dungarvan, together with lands in Desmond and Waterford, to Thomas FitzAnthony, for the yearly rent of 250 marks – about £165. Thereafter, ownership of the castle and royal manor of Dungarvan was closely bound up with possession of these other more extensive lands. In 1259 Henry III granted them to John FitzThomas FitzGerald, but at a rent of 500 marks a year, double the earlier sum and perhaps a sign of growing economic prosperity in the region. On FitzGerald's death in 1282, the estate was inherited by his cousin and heir, Thomas FitzMaurice.

The first clue that the manor of Dungarvan may already have contained a town dates from 1205, the year after King John acquired it. In that year, John is recorded as giving the Augustinian abbey of Greatconnell in County Kildare 'five burgages in Dungarvan'. This use of the word 'burgage' was significant. It was a precise legal term used only to describe property in settlements which had been granted status as a borough by the king or a feudal lord, and whose inhabitants in consequence enjoyed considerable legal and economic advantages. Thus at Dungarvan, the implication is that the king had already conferred such a grant on whatever settlement existed around the castle before 1205. The expectation was that it would mature into a successful market town under the influence of the economic freedoms and incentives the charter contained. Of course not every medieval settlement with a borough charter ultimately became a town. Some, located in impoverished and out of the way places, remained mere villages. But significantly, there were no towns in medieval Ireland which were not also boroughs.

At Dungarvan, King John seems to have been particularly concerned to ensure the economic success of the new borough, for ten years later, in 1215, he granted it a new and more advantageous charter. Like many others in Ireland, this was modelled on the laws of Breteuil, a Norman borough in France, which at this time was included among the English crown's possessions in that country. Among the rights this conferred on the people of Dungarvan was the right to a fixed annual rent of twelve pence for each building-plot or burgage and the freedom to dispose of their property at will. Moreover, strict limits were also laid down on the size of the economic obligations and financial penalties which their manorial lord – who at this time was still the king himself – could impose on them. Most importantly from the point of view of the townspeople, this meant that in future years, when the king had granted possession of the manor to the like of the FitzAnthonys and the FitzGeralds, these lords could do little to interfere in the running of Dungarvan's affairs. Some years later, in 1242, Henry III granted the town the right to hold an annual fair in the first week of August, specifically, as the grant says, for the improvement of the manor and, ultimately, for the king's own advantage. Fifty years later, the town generated rents worth over thirteen pounds a year. If we assume that each burgess was still paying twelve pence a year for his burgage plot in the town, this would indicate a rent-paying population of about 250 and a total population of at least four times that number.

The growth of medieval Dungarvan has left other traces in the modern town apart from the castle. Across the harbour at Abbeyside, the remains of the Augustinian friary founded in 1290 by Thomas, Lord Offaly, survive, incorporated into a Roman Catholic chapel built sometime in the 1820s. Within the town itself, it seems probable that the modern Anglican church of St Mary stands on the same site as the original medieval parish church. The present church was built in 1828 but incorporated part of an earlier church of about 1700. This in turn had been erected on the site of the chancel of the pre-reformation parish church. The ruined wall pierced by curious round windows which stands to the west of the modern building is probably all that remains of this medieval church. Unusually, this stood outside the medieval town walls. These were built sometime before 1463. They ran south from the castle along what is today the modern promenade called The Lookout, then west along the line of Emmet Street, before turning due north along St Augustine Street towards the Quay, where they turned due east to join the castle once again. These walls survived well into early modern times. They are depicted in a view of the town published in 1746 and on a map of the town drawn in 1760, but seem to have virtually disappeared by the 1840s. The walls had an important influence on how and when the town's plan developed. They enclosed the earliest core of the town, where the streets displayed a distinctive rudimentary form of planning. As this originally medieval part of the town was unaffected by the replanning in the nineteenth century, we may reasonably conclude that the modern streets here, that is Church Street, Main Street and St Augustine Street, together with the narrow lanes that run down to the Quay, are all survivals from the medieval plan.

Beyond the walls, any medieval or later development is likely to have been less regular, but was of course swept away by the duke of Devonshire's grand and formal redevelopment after 1803.

The reference in 1463 to Dungarvan's walls is contained in a murage grant. These grants were passed by act of the Dublin parliament and enabled towns to levy taxes on certain classes of goods traded at their markets. This was in order to raise money to build or maintain their town walls. These grants were widely used in the fourteenth and fifteenth centuries by the royal exchequer as a means of sharing the increasingly heavy cost imposed on the crown by the defence of the English lordship in Ireland. This was at a time when the lordship faced growing political, military and economic disruption. The Dungarvan grant is interesting, because it refers both to the ancient importance of the honour of Dungarvan and also to its present devastated condition. Although the grant blames this state of affairs on the actions of the 'king's enemies', it seems likely that there were other, perhaps more fundamental reasons for Dungarvan's gradual decline by this time. It is probable, for example, that the long-term limits to the town's earlier prosperity had already been pre-determined by its geographical location. To the west, Youghal provided a more accessible outport for the produce of much of the Blackwater valley. To the east, New Ross and Waterford monopolised much of the trade generated in the extensive heartlands of the colony via the Barrow and Suir rivers. In effect, Dungarvan's potential for growth had already been squeezed for many years by the competition from its better-located neighbours. Worse still, the natural harbour which was the basis of the town's early prosperity was also partly the cause of its subsequent decline. The harbour's position at the mouth of a river and at the head of a large and shallow bay encouraged it to silt up rapidly. This meant that as shipping technology improved and ships grew larger, so the harbour became progressively less suitable for them. The combined effect of all of this was already evident by 1300, ostensibly the heyday of the English lordship in Ireland. Dungarvan's contribution to the royal taxation of that year was 'fifteen hundred of fish, worth £15', compared to Youghal which paid £40 and five hundred of fish, and Waterford city which paid £66. Eight years later the Dublin parliament excused Dungarvan its failure to build a bridge over the River Colligan on the grounds of its poverty.

Dungarvan never again regained its early medieval importance. The twin themes of relative poverty and occasional crisis continued to dog its fortunes right up until the end of the eighteenth century. The town suffered badly during the Desmond rebellion – it was largely burned down in 1582 – and again during the mid-seventeenth-century civil wars. Dungarvan declared for the confederacy in 1641, was captured by the lord president of Munster the following year, and was then retaken by the confederates. They used it as one of their supply ports until it was recaptured by royalist forces under the command of Lord Inchiquin in 1647. Two years later, Dungarvan was captured by Cromwell. According to local tradition, its inhabitants were only saved from total destruction by the quick thinking of one Mrs Nagle, who drank Cromwell's health as he entered the town.

Such is the stuff of legend. What is transparently clear is that Dungarvan's trade remained at a relatively low level throughout this period. Its one major export, the cod and hake taken from the off-shore Nymph Bank, was a typical high-volume low-value primary product, and could never support the levels of prosperity sustained by the large volumes of more valuable goods traded through Youghal and Waterford. Thus the old trade differentials between these three ports remained. In 1683, for example, Youghal and Waterford each exported well over £50,000 worth of goods, whereas Dungarvan's total was barely £5,000. Few buildings survive in the modern town from this period, but one that does reflects this trade. The old market house, which stands at the eastern end of Main Street on the site of the old medieval market place, probably incorporates part of an earlier guild hall. This had been built before 1642 on the strength of the new charter granted to the town by James I in 1610. Similarly, the remains of the old building nearby, commonly referred to as St Garvin's church, are more likely to be part of a sixteenth-century merchant's house.

Throughout the eighteenth century, Dungarvan continued to function as a minor port, supported by its fishery and
small ship-building industry. The view of the town published in 1746 depicts a ramshackle collection of buildings
huddled behind the town walls – very much in accordance
with Ryland's later description. The stage was thus set for
the remarkable improvement in the town financed by the
fifth and sixth dukes of Devonshire between the act of union
in 1801 and the great reform act of 1832. The Devonshires
had acquired massive estates in Counties Cork and Waterford in 1748, on the marriage of Lady Charlotte Boyle, heiress of the fourth earl of Cork and Orrery, to Lord Hartington,
the future fourth duke. The property in Dungarvan formed
part of this inheritance by virtue of the fact that the manor
and castle of Dungarvan had been vested in the earl of Cork
in 1604. In 1775, the fifth duke commissioned Bernard Scalé,
a notable Anglo-French land surveyor, to map his Irish
estates. Scalé's survey of Dungarvan provides us with a
fascinating insight into the state of the duke's property there
some twenty-five years before it was redeveloped. In all, the
duke owned some twenty-eight acres of land in the town.
Most of this lay outside the walls between the two main
roads which, prior to the redevelopment, ran in parallel fashion towards Youghal and Cappoquin, roughly where Emmet
Street and O'Connell Street are today. The duke also owned
a small number of houses within the walls near the castle,
and along the banks of the Colligan and near the Anglican
church. Scalé's survey shows that for the most part the
duke's property consisted of the poorest sort of cabin built
around the edge of large communal gardens. The only slated
houses on the estate were those near the castle and along the
Cappoquin road outside the west gate. Twenty years later, in
1795, the agent described most of the duke's houses as being
'built of mud, covered in straw [and] mostly old'. Clearly, a
greater contrast could hardly have existed between these
neglected and semi-ruinous hovels and the houses that were
shortly to replace them.

The decision to improve the Devonshire property in

Dungarvan was part of a broader strategy originally conceived in 1792, which was designed to re-assert the fifth duke's financial and political authority over his Irish estates. This had effectively been lost through the gross mismanagement of the previous agent, William Conner. On his enforced resignation in 1792, he was unable to account for nearly £15,000 of the duke's rents, and was suspected of every sort of duplicity and malpractice. The early efforts at improvement were concentrated at Lismore, and nothing was achieved at Dungarvan prior to the act of union in 1801. The passage of the act of course gave added urgency to the question of political control, since it involved a reduction in the number of Irish parliamentary seats by two-thirds and the transfer of the remainder to the imperial parliament in London. Dungarvan was one of the thirty-three borough seats which survived this process, and its correspondingly enhanced political importance after 1801 was recognised by the duke and his advisers alike.

The agent who re-established the duke's parliamentary control of Dungarvan was Thomas Knowlton, the second of Conner's English replacements. The problems he faced in doing so were formidable. The duke was only one of several landowners in the town, and as we have seen, his property there was much divided. The other landlords, including the marquis of Waterford, were not his natural political allies, and were generally tory whereas he was a whig. Moreover, his tenants were for the most part impoverished fishermen, and were ineligible under the existing property qualifications to vote. Dungarvan was one of the five post-union boroughs with a property qualification for the franchise. Only householders in the borough with property worth more than five pounds a year and freeholders in the manor worth more than forty shillings a year were entitled to vote. Finally, it was not altogether certain that the duke could yet regain possession of his property in the town. Many of the leases held by his tenants depended on the life of a Mr Roberts, who had gone to America thirty years previously and had not been heard of since. Knowlton's solution was to assume that Roberts had subsequently died, and persuade the tenants to attorn their property to the duke.

Knowlton's political strategy was three-fold. He first attempted an unlikely alliance with the tory marquis but this ended in predictable failure and defeat for the duke's candidate at the general election of 1802. His second tactic, begun the following year, was to embark on the politically judicious programme of urban renewal which has left such a profound mark on the centre of Dungarvan today. By providing employment, improving the town's amenities and bolstering its economy, Knowlton intended to raise the townspeople's expectations of the duke and attach them firmly to his politics. Initially all went well. By 1806, Devonshire Square (later Grattan Square), Bridge Street, Cross Bridge Street and William Street (later St Mary's Street) had been laid out, and the contracts agreed for the construction of the first houses around them. In October of the same year Knowlton described at length the progress that had been made:

> The best situations for building in this town belong to his grace. They form a sort of nucleus or core in the centre of the town. These I found covered by a parcel of mud cabins in ruins, not one of them good enough to give the occupier a vote ... I saw that it might be converted into the best part of the town; that it might all be made valuable building ground, and to give the duke a decided preponderance in the borough; and that, if he built on it himself, he might keep command of what he created ...
>
> A great quantity of the best materials of timber, Welsh slate, Yorkshire flags and Portland stone for fireplaces and hearths have been imported from England, at a much cheaper rate than must have been given for materials of very inferior quality, had they been purchased in Ireland. A central square and several streets have been laid out by erecting register pillars and contracts have been made for building twelve houses for the inferior sort immediately, but which will all create good votes for the borough. I have determined on the building houses of this description first, with a view to offer them to such of the deserving and industrious inhabitants of the old cabins as may appear to deserve them, which we must throw down to make our new streets and openings. [This was] a measure which humanity dictated and does not appear impolitic. I thought I was acting consistently with the duke of Devonshire's character and would rather raise his popularity.
>
> To this state we have advanced our progress and it has caused a revolution in the public sentiment in respect to his grace's power ... It has set men's minds a-speculating and roving. Some expect they may be favoured with a good house, others that they may obtain

*profits by being employed or by selling something during the erection of these buildings, which their opposition would deprive them of; in short, that they may come in for something, although they have no determinate idea of what.*

The tactic seemed to work. In the general election of 1806, the duke's candidate, General George Walpole, was returned for the borough.

Knowlton and his successors continued this policy of investing in public projects in the town over the next twenty years. On their advice, the duke gave the site for the present Roman Catholic church in 1815 together with a later grant of £1,500 towards its completion. He constructed the bridge over the Colligan between 1810 and 1816, and built the new quays at the harbour in the late 1820s. In all, the fifth and sixth dukes of Devonshire together spent over £71,000 on Dungarvan between 1803 and 1830, but not all of it on these sorts of public project. The fifth duke and his advisers soon realised that 'buying' political support in this way was an expensive business. Once begun, it was difficult to stop. It had to be pretty well continuous, or else voters were quickly seduced by the promises of rival candidates. For example at the election of 1807, General Walpole only narrowly defeated the marquis of Waterford's candidate, Colonel Keane, largely because Knowlton had allowed the work of rebuilding to come to a halt, thus raising doubts among the voters about the duke's true intentions.

The lesson was quickly learnt and Knowlton and his successors supplemented this public investment with a third tactic. Between 1811 and 1830, they built nearly four hundred small cabins on the southern edge of the town at Black-pool and Boreheenatra. These were for the express purpose of increasing the number of voters who would support the duke's candidate. By leasing each cabin for the duration of the life of one named person – not the would-be tenant – the duke's agent created a new vote in the borough. By specifying the name of an elderly person as the life on each lease, the agent ensured that the tenant would probably have to renew his lease quite soon, and thereby gave him every incentive to remain loyal to the duke's candidate. Most of these tenants were fishermen, who also needed a small plot of land on which to dry their catch. As a further inducement to political fidelity, these plots were rented to them separately on a year-to-year basis. This time the tactic worked supremely well. Despite the marquis of Waterford's attempt to do precisely the same thing on his own property in the town, the sixth duke simply out-built him. Accordingly, the duke retained political control of Dungarvan until the reform act of 1832, when he withdrew from further active intervention in Irish politics because of his support for reform and his growing distaste at the increasing violence of Irish elections.

Twenty-seven years later, the Devonshires withdrew from Dungarvan entirely. When the sixth duke died in 1858, he left debts of over a million pounds. As part of an urgent general attempt at retrenchment by the family, the Devonshire property in Dungarvan was sold through the landed estates court to the sitting tenants for £29,500 between 1859 and 1861.

The link between the duke of Devonshire and Dungarvan was thereby broken, but its legacy survives. Admittedly, Devonshire Square has become Grattan Square, and William Street is now St Mary Street, but much of the urban fabric and the sense of 'urban space' which survives today is the duke's creation. This is partly because the town experienced little growth in later years. Indeed, as in so many other provincial towns in Ireland, its population actually fell in the later nineteenth century from 8,600 in 1841 to 4,900 in 1901. At around 6,000 its present population is still only three-quarters of what it was in the pre-famine years. Thus today, if you walk from Abbeyside, over the bridge along Bridge Street and into Grattan Square, and look up St Mary Street towards the Catholic church at its focal point, you can still experience something of the coherence and scale of the urban vision of the fifth and sixth dukes, and their agents and architects. Walk out along O'Connell Street or Emmet Street and you come across a surprising number of the cabins built during the political duel between the duke and the marquis; modernised perhaps, but still recognisable for what they were. Walk east along Main Street towards the old market house, or down the lanes towards the quay and you walk back through time towards the medieval origins of the town. But wherever you walk, you are surrounded by the urban past and reminded of its importance in shaping today's urban present.

**Select bibliography**

W. Fraher: *Dungarvan. An Architectural Inventory*, Dungarvan, 1984
W. Fraher: 'The reconstruction of Dungarvan, 1807–c. 1830. A political ploy', *Decies*, xxv (1984 ), pp. 5-10
L. J. Proudfoot: 'Landlord motivation and urban improvement on the duke of Devonshire's Irish estates, *c*.1792–1832', *Irish Economic and Social History*, xviii (1991), pp. 5-23

# MULLINGAR

## J. H. Andrews

A DISTINGUISHED geographer, the late T. W. Freeman, addressing an audience of university students through the medium of an advanced academic textbook on the geography of Ireland, wrote: 'A love of beauty, so characteristic of many Mediterranean peoples, is hardly obvious in Ireland, for most of the towns are ugly except where the Georgian imprint remains, and even the churches are with some significant exceptions surprisingly unattractive.' 'Ugly' is fighting talk by any standards; and notice how Freeman makes matters worse by praising an architectural style named after an English king and by levelling the word 'unattractive' at just those buildings that Irishmen of all faiths would regard as most inviting. We can of course reply that ugliness is in the eye of the beholder. The fact remains that Irish towns have been similarly condemned by many other observers, and especially by newcomers driving through the countryside for the first time. I certainly felt that way about them when I was a newcomer nearly forty years ago.

So what else can be said in rebuttal? One cure for ugliness is antiquity. The 'significant exceptions' to the rule of ecclesiastical ugliness in the passage I have just quoted are surely our medieval churches. An old building or an old landscape, especially if it is known to be old, becomes somehow at once mellow, romantic, dignified and (a word that means both old and dignified) venerable. A second cure for ugliness is familiarity. Which of us has an ugly mother? The traveller who stays in his car has failed to familiarise himself. Speeding westwards from Dublin through a town like Mullingar, for example, he probably won't notice more than one street as he drives past the water tower, down the hill, across the canal, between the shops, across the canal again, and so on towards Athlone with no lasting impression in his mind but shop-fronts, traffic lights, and other people's cars. Our

*Mullingar, market square in 1870, courtesy of Royal Irish Academy*

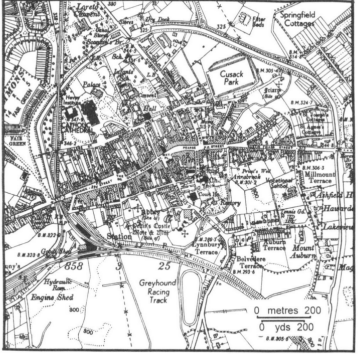

*Mullingar 1953, Ordnance Survey of Ireland, 1:2500*

hypothetical traveller should park his car and start walking, not through the town but in the town. The more he sees of the back streets the better he will like the main street; and he will finish by liking the back streets as well, provided he takes enough time to acquire what is admittedly an acquired taste.

Antiquity and familiarity both involve the blending of space and time, on different scales and in the present context with different practical implications. I cannot make you familiar with Mullingar in one short article but at least I can show the town to be considerably older than it seems.

Ireland is famous for its ruins, and most of our historic towns contain some visible proof of being historic, such as old castles, churches, abbeys, walls, gatehouses and so on. The town I have been asked to discuss is a strange exception to this rule, as we can see at once by asking: what is the oldest building in Mullingar? This can be a difficult question anywhere in Ireland, because on the whole our towns have very few historical documents, and even fewer historians to read them. In Mullingar it is more difficult than usual because most of the town appears to be of nineteenth-century date, and none of it *looks* older than the nineteenth century.

So what *was* the oldest building in Mullingar? That's not so difficult. It must be the mill that gave the town its name, the mill on which St Colman exercised his miraculous powers in the seventh century by making its wheel turn in the wrong direction. Obviously this mill preceded the rest of the settlement, because no complex entity like a town is named by describing one of its constituent parts. So this is the oldest man-made landmark that a time-traveller could hope to see – we must say 'man-made' because the mill was clearly not so old as the stream that drove it. The motorist may be aware of going first downhill and then uphill as he passes from Austin Friars Street into Pearse Street, but he will almost certainly miss the river that flows under the road at its lowest point. Even a pedestrian may miss it. Yet the Brosna is historically the dominant natural feature in the town: narrow, shallow, obviously unnavigable, but vigorous and even dangerous, capable of closing whole streets with its floods. In modern times the river at Mullingar has never been famous for its mills, but two did survive until the nineteenth century: Friar's Mill beside the Royal Canal, and the Mount Mill less than half a mile downstream, both sites devoid of industrial buildings today, but both identifiable from their old mill races. The physical fabric of a mill-house is unlikely to last very long by a historian's standards, but the same mill stream may turn a succession of wheels for many centuries, and either of these sites could conceivably date back to when the first water-mills were introduced to Ireland in Early Christian times. Everyone in Mullingar knows all about St Colman, but who can show us where his miracle took place? The only way to choose between the two most likely possibilities is by their names. The friars commemorated in the Friar's Mill were evidently the Dominicans, and they didn't reach Mullingar until the thirteenth century. Anyone can own a mill without having built it, but many thirteenth-century monastic orders did build themselves mills, so perhaps we can assume that this is what happened here. Which leaves the Mount Mill as the most probable site for St Colman and the right place to begin our walk.

The mount, like the mill, has long since ceased to exist, but it appears on the earliest surviving map of Mullingar, drawn in 1691, overlooking the mill site somewhere near the present county offices at the lower end of Mount Street, and it was evidently one of those small but steep-sided artificial hills or mottes built in the late twelfth century by the Anglo-Norman ruling class. This motte belonged to William Petit, first lord of the manor of Mullingar. Later it became the king's castle of Mullingar, another building that has left no trace. No doubt Petit wished to command the site of what now became the manorial mill, but his motte was too far down the valley slope to command the town of Mullingar – presumably because when he built the motte there wasn't a town of Mullingar.

But the town certainly followed soon afterwards, and our next landmark in chronological order is its main street, as represented today by Pearse Street and Oliver Plunkett Street. It is unlikely that William Petit himself laid out this street across a green field. More probably it was a pre-Norman country road, because like most ancient roads it varies unpredictably in width and alignment whereas streets designed to accommodate town houses are usually straight and uniformly wide. In fact the curve of this street, and its relation to the slope of the Brosna valley, are still a most attractive feature, allowing the town to unfold itself in stages to the visitor's eye instead of appearing all at once in a single view. What the Normans did was lay out plots of building land on either side of this older central axis, and some at least of the boundaries between those plots still serve their original purpose. The first houses have been rebuilt many times, leaving today a varied assortment of roof lines, facades, fenestrations and shop-fronts, some twentieth-century, many Victorian, a few late Georgian – though nothing that our textbook author would call a 'Georgian imprint' – and none pre-Georgian. For a long time Mullingar people have been too busy putting up new buildings to spare much thought for the preservation of old ones. It certainly takes an effort of the imagination to picture the main street before the time of Oliver Cromwell when its population was partly Anglo-Norman and partly Gaelic Irish, both groups living mainly in thatched houses and both with a few privileged families in small castles.

And before the reformation both groups would have worshipped in the same parish church. At least that still exists, though no longer in its medieval form. It was rebuilt in the nineteenth century to look like a medieval church, perhaps in the hope of implying historical continuity between medieval and Protestant Christianity. What this church does achieve is topographical continuity, for surely its thirteenth-century predecessor was on the same site, a spur above the Brosna about a hundred yards south of the main street, chosen perhaps because the street was already lined with settlers' building-plots before the church was built.

So far we have found few signs of urban activity in medieval Mullingar. Mills, mottes, castles, main streets and parish churches are just as common in villages as in towns. Technically, it is true, Mullingar could claim to be a borough, in the sense of possessing legal privileges appropriate to a town, at least as early as 1297, but so were many other places in medieval Ireland that never grew into real towns and were probably never expected to. To judge the success of any one such settlement we must compare it with other settlements in the same region. Mullingar lay in a belt of strong Norman influence still recognisable today by the number of surviving mottes and castles and the high density of English or half-English place-names such as Robinstown, Walshestown, Marlinstown and Hopestown. This zone stretched from the east coast of Ireland to Lough Ree, becoming narrower with increasing distance from Dublin as it forced its way between the native territories of Offaly on the south and Annaly on the north. A network of towns was a strategic necessity to link the heartlands of Meath and Kildare with the Shannon crossing, but the only places that made much progress in this western heartland were Athlone, Ballymore, Kilbixy, Kilbeggan and Mullingar. At first Kilbixy, some eight miles north-west of Mullingar, seemed to be taking the lead. Tradition described it as a place of great note, with a mayor and twelve burgesses clad in scarlet gowns, and with the ruins of many ancient houses and castles still recognisable in the seventeenth century. Tradition also tells how at some unspecified time a market cross was ceremonially uprooted from Kilbixy and carried across those eight miles to be replanted. Its new home had two advantages that no alternative site could match. It was centrally placed within the Anglo-Norman salient. And it was also what the old geography books used to call a gap town, where routeways are forced to converge upon a narrow funnel through some physical barrier. The barrier here ran more or less from north to south and was formed mainly by Lough Owel and Lough Ennell. The effective gap between the lakes was narrower than it looks on the map because much of it was too boggy to be crossed by roads until the eighteenth century. In fact in about fourteen miles distance there were less than two miles with a clear east-west passage, a space now wholly given over to urbanisation.

Besides being equidistant from the northern and southern Norman frontiers Mullingar also became central between east and west in 1543 when Westmeath was detached from Meath and created a separate county, the first move in a prolonged attempt by England's Tudor dynasty to modernise the government of Ireland. So on grounds of position alone it was natural that Mullingar should now be named as shire town of County Westmeath. It also had a building that could conveniently be used as county jail. This was the Dominican friary, now long since vanished needless to say, which had recently been closed by Henry VIII on the southwest outskirts of the town. After the further pacification of Ireland in the seventeenth century the status of county capital was to furnish Mullingar with most of its largest public buildings as local government bodies extended their functions from the administration of justice to the collection of taxes, the maintenance of roads and bridges, the provision of public health care, the making of maps and surveys, and the preservation of records. By late Victorian times the town was ringed with gaunt grey institutional presences – a jail, a courthouse, an infirmary (sometimes regarded as the oldest extant building in the town, though it cannot be older than the 1770s), an asylum, a workhouse with its nearby cemetery, and – since local government had to be backed by force – a barracks. Some writers have condemned these structures as symbolic of colonial oppression, but the British government was building plenty of others in Britain at the same period.

As a borough Mullingar had the right to hold markets and fairs, but it was not until the time of Sir Henry Piers in 1682 that anyone had much to say about its trading activities. Then, Piers tells us, the town was 'a great thoroughfare or road from Dublin to Connacht. All the houses are alehouses', he adds, 'yet some of the richer sort drive at other trades also; they sell all sorts of commodities to the gentry abroad in the country, and some besides have large farms abroad.' The word 'rich', even if only in the comparative degree, is an impressive label for the people of any small Irish community, and to write of 'driving at' a trade suggests an unusual level of commercial vigour. And these traders handled 'all sorts' of commodities – not just the usual small-town staples of ale, tobacco, salt and iron. And the farms they had in the surrounding area were 'large', larger evidently than the usual paddocks and townparks. But none of this prosperity left much material expression. Piers does admit that Mullingar's modern houses were 'better' than the old castles, but then changes his mind and substitutes 'more commodious', perhaps simply meaning that they had larger windows and not so many awkward stairs. In fact we know from the report of a fire that destroyed the town in 1747 that most of the houses then still had thatched roofs.

The most profitable commodities sold in Mullingar were cattle, sheep and horses – a fact first hinted at by the exceptionally large area of common grazing land adjacent to the town recorded in mid-seventeenth-century surveys. Most of the commons seem to have disappeared soon after 1661. That was the year in which Mullingar ceased to be a borough – nobody knows why, but it may have been to give more power to its new landlord, Sir Arthur Forbes, later Lord Granard, as a way of rewarding his special loyalty to King Charles II. The town was now the only manor in Ireland with its own member of parliament, but manorial status no longer meant very much. What mattered now were the business relations between a proprietor and his individual tenants. The Granards were absentee landlords with their home and most of their estate in County Longford. They never made Mullingar an estate town in any architectural or topographical sense. In fact their main achievement was to appropriate the commons, to divide them into separate farms, and to collect rents from them. The only fragments that escaped were the fair green at the western end of the town and two small market places adjoining the main street: here the Granard family collected not rents but tolls, but they did also build a market house which was handsomely rebuilt by their successor Lord Greville and which is still well maintained as offices and a museum. Enclosing the commons did not affect the town's economy. On the contrary its fairs became steadily busier until they ranked second only to those of Ballinasloe, attracting dealers from all over Ireland as well as from Britain and the continent, spilling out of the fair green into the main streets, and causing serious problems of dirt, congestion and law-enforcement. Today's livestock are sold in a purpose-built market unseen by casual visitors, but part of Lord Granard's old fair green can still be identified as an open space.

Trade is impossible without transport facilities, but Mullingar had no navigable river and by the eighteenth century its traffic had outgrown the narrow winding roads inherited from medieval times. Other towns had an industrial revolution. Other counties had an agricultural revolution. Modern Mullingar is a monument to no less than three transport revolutions. First in the 1730s came the turnpike system whose legacy here is the wide straight roads that now approach the town from both east and west. As it happened, the main effect of the turnpikes was to improve a competing road through Kinnegad, Kilbeggan and Moate and so leave Mullingar detached from central Ireland's principal line of movement between Dublin and Galway. But the town did benefit from better links with Dublin, Lanesborough and Longford, especially after a castle and other centrally placed buildings were knocked down in 1826 to make a new passage for the Longford coaches along what now became Castle Street.

A rule in the historical geography of transport is that to him that hath shall be given. It was illustrated in 1806 when the Royal Canal Company brought navigable water to Mullingar, despite severe technical difficulties, in expectation of the revenue that a town of three to four thousand people might be expected to generate. The canal brought coal and building materials to Mullingar, sent corn and livestock products out, and until the coming of the railway carried passengers in both directions. Its northward horseshoe curve around the town was a partial adjustment to the local contour lines, but a massive embankment was still needed to cross the Brosna valley and a deep cutting to penetrate the adjacent ridge. The canal harbour is now deserted and most of the storehouses have gone the way of other historic buildings in Mullingar, but a walk along the towpath is rich in visual content and gives a clear impression of the town's topographical unity. The same is true, to a lesser extent and more fleetingly, for railway passengers perched above the Brosna floodplain to the south of the town, though this feeling soon evaporates when the passengers disembark. Mullingar was once proud of its Victorian railway station and especially of the refreshment rooms set exactly in the angle between the Galway and Sligo branches. Today you can still catch a train, but there is no refreshment for either body or aesthetic sense. Here is one corner of Mullingar that failed to mellow with advancing age.

Roads, canals and railways all allowed the town to maintain its position as a trading centre – and to regain a measure of self-government when town commissioners were appointed in 1856 – but they did nothing to diversify its industrial structure beyond the basic Irish urban endowment of forges, tanneries and breweries. In the nineteenth century powerful economic forces were concentrating the nation's industry in the larger seaports, and driving much of it through the seaports and across the channel into Britain. It took the industrial policies of the post-independence era and the coming of motor transport to give Mullingar its present quota of manufacturing jobs and a present total population of about 10,000.

The last of our landmarks, the Catholic Cathedral of Christ the King, is also the most visible. Everywhere in Ireland the reformation left parish churches in the hands of a small religious minority which in Mullingar came to consist mainly of professional men, public servants, soldiers from the barracks, and gentlemen from nearby country houses – altogether a group strong and wealthy enough to keep All Saints' church in good repair and even to give it a fine nineteenth-century spire, but never comprising more than ten per cent of the population. For nearly two hundred years after the reformation, Catholics worshipped in obscurity, their first identifiable mass-house (to use the derogatory jargon of the time) being insalubriously located in the drying room of a local tannery. The first proper chapel was hidden away on the northern edge of the town, beside a narrow and little-frequented passage then known as Back of the Town or Back Lane. As topographical terms 'back', and its implied correlative 'front', are far from self-explanatory. In this case they suggest what might be called an ascendancy viewpoint somewhere near the king's castle, the courthouse or the Protestant church. Yet by accident the 'back of the town' includes the highest land in Mullingar, a fact eventually exploited with increasing self-confidence by successive Catholic churches near its summit, culminating in the enormous present-day cathedral, now over fifty years old and just beginning to benefit from the rule that antiquity makes the eye grow fonder. Around this site has grown a Catholic institutional quarter including two convents, two schools, a bishop's palace and an assembly hall. In its vicinity, low-grade housing has been removed, trees and bushes planted, and streets given more dignified names. Despite its marginal position in a spatial sense, this is clearly the heart of Mullingar and a fitting place at which to close our tour.

But not, I hope, to close the study of local history. To analyse any town into a collection of landmarks is really a great mistake, to be tolerated only in circumstances of exceptional difficulty such as the delivering of a lecture. The true urban historian should give most of his attention to overall topographical structure: to the pattern of all the streets, in this case nearly two hundred of them; of all the buildings, large and small, public and private, residential and non-residential; and of all the gardens, yards, open spaces and watercourses – including the underground watercourses that gave so much worry to the public health authorities of nineteenth-century Mullingar. Such patterns are beyond the capacity of sound radio. They need maps, pictures and diagrams – just what the Royal Irish Academy is now providing, along with much detailed written comment, in its *Irish Historic Towns Atlas*, to which the present talks may be regarded as complementary.

189

## Select bibiliography

H. Piers: 'A chorographical description of the county of West-Meath', in C. Vallancey (ed.), *Collectanea de rebus Hibernicis*, i, 1770

T. Conlon: 'The sunny side of old Mullingar', *Westmeath Examiner*, 19 April 1947 – 28 June 1959

J. Brady: *The Parish of Mullingar*, Mullingar, 1962

Westmeath County Council, *Mullingar Development Plan*, 1986

P. O'Farrell: *The Book of Mullingar*, Mullingar, 1987

J. H. Andrews with K. M. Davies: 'Mullingar', *Irish Historic Towns Atlas*, no. 5, Dublin, 1992

# LIST OF CONTRIBUTORS

*Professor J. H. Andrews*

Geography Department,
Trinity College, Dublin

*Professor R. H. Buchanan*

Institute of Irish Studies,
Belfast

*Dr W. H. Crawford*

Federation for Ulster Local
Studies, Belfast

*Mrs Mary Davies*

Royal Irish Academy,
Dublin

*Dr Harman Murtagh*

Regional Technical College,
Athlone

*Dr Arnold Horner*

Geography Department,
University College, Dublin

*Dr Margart MacCurtain*

Department of Modern
Irish History, University
College, Dublin

*Dr William Nolan*

Geography Department,
University College, Dublin

*Dr Mary O'Dowd*

School of Modern History,
Queen's University, Belfast

*Professor Patrick O'Flanagan*

Geography Department,
University College, Cork

*Dr L. J. Proudfoot*

School of Geosciences,
Queen's University, Belfast

*Dr Philip Robinson*            Ulster Folk and Transport
                               Museum, Cultragh, Belfast

*Professor Anngret Simms*       Geography Department,
                               University College, Dublin

*Dr Kevin Whelan*               Royal Irish Academy,
                               Dublin